# RECOVERY ROAD TRIP

# RECOVERY ROAD TRIP

*Finding Purpose*
*and*
*Connection*
*on the Journey Home*

## PATTI CLARK

SHE WRITES PRESS

Published 2024
Printed in the United States of America
Print ISBN: 978-1-64742-774-0
E-ISBN: 978-1-64742-775-7
Library of Congress Control Number: 2024909096
For information, address:
She Writes Press
1569 Solano Ave #546
Berkeley, CA 94707

*Interior design by Stacey Aaronson*

She Writes Press is a division of SparkPoint Studio, LLC.

*This book is dedicated to my wonderful sons, Lukas and Devin.*
*I love you both with all of my heart and soul.*

*Author's Note*

This book is a story, an allegorical narrative, but it is born out of my own experience and that of other women in recovery that I interviewed. I believe deeply that communicating through story is the most powerful way to communicate experience. I am a middle-aged woman in recovery. Because of my own dissatisfaction and frustration with some experiences in 12-Step recovery, mostly due to some of the people I encountered, I left recovery after almost thirteen years of sobriety. I was out in the "normal" world for almost thirteen years before finding my way back in. During my time out in that world and then back in "the rooms," I met so many women, personally and online, who have had similar experiences. The interviews and conversations that I've shared with these women ultimately led me to write this book.

Part of my experience (and the experience of others) after leaving recovery, and even after returning, was a feeling of stuck-ness, a feeling of frustration and grief, wondering "Is this all there is?" That stuck feeling, that overwhelming feeling of fear and grief, led me to do a lot of research and learn vital things that helped me get unstuck. So, my recovery was not only in 12-Step, my journey to and in recovery has encompassed several other modalities, including therapeutic work to release trauma patterning, self-empowerment through exploring the sacred feminine, and many other areas, which I explore in this book.

Although this is fiction, it still encompasses my story and the story of women I spoke to. I believe that a lot of women will see their story here too. I wrote this book in the hope that it will speak to other women, perhaps help them to not make the same mistakes I did, and help them decide to find their own path to recovery, or stay in recovery until they find the connections they need.

This book is divided into two distinct sections. Part One is the allegorical narrative that I described above, and Part Two is about helping people embark upon their own healing journey through journaling. The journaling notebook follows the journey of the protagonist and allows the reader to explore her own inner journey.

# CONTENTS

**PART TWO**
Recovery Road Trip: The Workbook

# PART ONE

*Meg's Journey*

## CHAPTER 1

# *Victimhood*

SEATTLE, WA

---

*"This above all, refuse to be a victim."*
—MARGARET ATWOOD

ight filtered through branches as I navigated my way through the redwoods en route to Seattle from California. My mind drifted as I drove north. It had been a rough couple of weeks. I had been back in my hometown to bury my father.

My father died a broken man, a raging alcoholic. My mother had been dead for over twenty years, so although I had been estranged from him for most of my adult life, as the only child, the post-death details were left to me. So I found myself in California cleaning up the mess that had been his life.

I was hoping he'd left a bit of an estate, a surprise gift after a shitty childhood. Alas, it was not to be. After I met with his lawyer, I found out that he did indeed leave everything to me—especially his bills and his chaos. After cleaning out his house and selling what I could, but trashing most of it, and after selling the house and paying off the bills and the second and third mortgages, there wasn't much left. I ended up with a few thousand dollars and his car, an old Ford Mustang that looked much the worse for wear. But at least it ran.

Before my dad died, although my life was ticking along fine, I felt empty and lost a lot of the time. When I talked to friends, I asked them how they found fulfillment. That feeling of accomplishment seemed so elusive. I often found myself going through the motions at work and looking around and wondering if the people I worked with felt joy at being alive. My colleagues often told me to "cheer up" and asked "why the long face?" I hated that. It seemed like I was the only one who didn't know how to do life correctly. I had been sober for over five years, but I was feeling stagnant and stuck. Even my recovery didn't feel as life-affirming as it once did.

So I decided to take the time I had after the funeral to do some self-exploration. I would take my newly inherited car and drive up from California to Seattle to stay with my dear friend Nella. I was in no hurry to get back to New Zealand, where I now lived. It was July, beautiful summer weather for a drive up the Pacific coast, but dismal winter back home. I had taken time off work, and I didn't have to rush back. My sons were grown and in college back in NZ, and being divorced, I had no partner impatiently awaiting my return. I was a free agent and I needed some time to sort things out.

I stayed close to the sea as much as possible on the drive up through northern California and Oregon, occasionally taking side roads so that I could stop and sit by the water, watching the light sparkling on its surface. The Pacific had always soothed me. I needed that kind of comfort now, in the wake of my dad's death, as memories came rushing in. The first thing I remembered when I thought of him was his harsh, critical voice, which often resided in my head— the voice that told me that I could do better, that I wasn't trying hard enough, that I was taking the easy way out. Or the one that told me that I just wasn't good enough . . . I remembered with a sigh what he said to my first boyfriend . . . "Any port in a storm, huh?" It wasn't a huge surprise that I lacked confidence and faith in myself. It was while I was sitting by the ocean, contemplating that pain in the midst of so much beauty, that I decided that I just could not keep living in this state of joylessness; I realized that I needed to do something radical to change my life.

"Oh, honey, you look exhausted," Nell said as I fell into her arms when I finally arrived at her house well after 10:00 p.m.

We talked for a while before I went to bed, but I was having a hard time keeping my eyes open. I briefly told her a bit about my trip, how good it felt to drive up the coast, to have no agenda, and have some space and time for myself.

Nella put me to bed in her spare room and rubbed my back as tears ran down my cheeks. She kissed my forehead in a very maternal way, and I felt safer and more loved than I had in many years. I fell asleep almost instantly.

The next morning, after pouring myself a cup of coffee from the never-empty coffee pot in Nella's kitchen, I slowly made my way down to Nella's studio, still feeling stiff and tired from the long drive the day before.

Nella was an amazing artist: She painted, she sculpted, she gardened, she cooked, she sewed . . . and she mended hearts. The last was her greatest quality, and one of the main reasons that I came to her house to heal.

Nella's studio was in her old garage. After she bought her house, Nella had her brother come and stay with her, and together they transformed her garage into an amazing studio space with huge windows, open and airy. She always had a few canvases on the go, and a kiln in one corner where she fired her pottery. That particular morning, as I walked into the studio, Nella was placing some small sculptures, recently out of the kiln, on a shelf.

"Ah, you're up and you've got coffee. I'm so glad you slept. I was hoping you'd be able to sleep in; you looked pretty ragged last night," she said as she placed the last piece on the shelf. "I could use more coffee myself. Let's go up to the kitchen so we can talk."

We walked back up to the house together, and Nella propped the back door open so the sun could stream in. As she poured us each a cup of coffee, I heard the birds chirping and watched as they feasted at the feeder that Nella kept full. She collected the feathers that the different birds sometimes left for her in her yard, and she had them strategically placed around her house, along with her pottery, some old bones she had gathered from the beach, and her plethora of plants.

"Thank you so much for letting me stay here," I said as I stifled a yawn. "I wish I could just move in. I love it here. I don't ever want to leave."

"You *can* move in . . . Stay!" Nella exclaimed, and I knew she meant it.

"Oh, Nell, I wish I could. I dread going home to be honest. If it weren't for the boys, I'd move in tomorrow. I feel kind of homeless and hopeless at the moment.

I feel like shit. Not only because of Dad, you know we weren't close, but his death still feels like a real ending. Even though I'm well past being a kid, I still feel like an orphan. And more than that, I was hoping I'd feel some closure, feel something different. But I don't."

I got up and poured myself more coffee, gathering my thoughts, and leaned against the counter. "But it's more than that. I've lost my excitement about life. I just feel completely stuck. I know that part of that is because both of my boys are out of the house now; my huge role of motherhood is gone. Trust me, I've read a lot about empty-nest syndrome. But all my old patterns of behavior seem to be keeping me trapped and so damned unfulfilled. I don't feel like I'm progressing at all. I feel like I'm so limited in my choices and opportunities for change, and I just don't know how to get unstuck."

I took a sip of coffee and stared out the window. "When I got into recovery the first time, I thought that that was the answer. I felt all glowy, like I was shining from the inside out, and starting a new life. And you know how much therapy I did after I got sober, trying to deal with all the shit that I was drinking not to feel. I thought, *Well after all that work, now I must be all better; now I can start having this amazing life.* But you know, life just sort of carries on, the shimmer was gone and life got hard. So you know my story, I went out and started drinking again . . . and life got harder. I knew that wasn't the answer. So I got back into recovery, and I'm really glad I did. I know my life is much better without drugs and alcohol. But it still feels . . . oh, I don't know. . . I just feel flat and purposeless. How do other people do it? What is their secret?" I sighed and gulped more coffee. I tended to drink coffee the way I used to drink wine, thinking more caffeine might be the answer.

Nella didn't try to fix me; that was one of the many things I loved about her. She just listened intently and nodded. I didn't feel judged about not doing it right, nor pity, which I could not tolerate.


Later that morning, I went for a walk at the estuary near where Nella lived. On my way back to the house, while I was waiting to cross the street, a car drove by with the bumper sticker: "Life's a Bitch and Then You Die." And I thought: *Yeah that's it. What's the point to all of this? We struggle, we suffer, and then we die.*

When I got back to the house, Nella had gone off to run some errands, but there was a small clay figure of a fig on the table on top of a piece of paper with my name on it. I held the small clay fig in the palm of my hand and felt a lightness start to glow inside. Nella knew how I felt about figs; I've always loved them. They are so utterly female. I read something in college that in some ancient culture, the fig was associated with female genitalia. I used to pontificate about figs after a few drinks at parties when I was young; I would joke that if you split a fig open, it had a definite vulvic vibe. And I'd explain to anyone that would listen that the Greek word for fig is the same as the word for vulva (*sykon*), and in Italian, the word for fig (*fica*) is slang for vagina. "And so," I would say, "I rest my case." It used to be a joke between Nella and me, when we were feeling powerful and womanly, we'd say we felt "Figgy." No one knew what we meant, and we liked that; it was our secret code word.

Nella had painted me a big fig several years earlier; it resembled the back of a woman with bare buttocks staring out to sea. It was whimsical and fun, but sensual and spiritual, too, like an image of the Divine Feminine in fruit form. I had once read this description of the sacred feminine by the Christian Mystic Saint Hildegard, and I had started thinking of my fig painting as this goddess: "She is so bright and glorious that you cannot look at her face or her garments for the splendor with which she shines. For she is terrible with the terror of the avenging lightning, and gentle with the goodness of the bright sun; and both her terror and her gentleness are incomprehensible to humans. . . . But she is with everyone and in everyone, and so beautiful is her secret that no person can know the sweetness with which she sustains people, and spares them in inscrutable mercy."

I went to bed early that night, holding my little fig statue and thinking about my Goddess Fig. I went to sleep thinking that I was missing something important and that time was escaping somehow. I didn't want to end up on my deathbed saying, "Life's a bitch and then you die."

I stumbled into the kitchen, rubbing my eyes, and poured myself some coffee.

"I didn't sleep so great last night," I said, stifling a yawn. I sat down across from Nell and took a long sip of coffee. "Oh, Nell, I feel so scared, like I'm wasting my life. I mean, we're not getting any younger, and I just don't like my life. I feel like I'm just sleepwalking through it most of the time. My dad's death has been a real wake up call. I don't want to die and feel like I wasted time waiting for my real life to begin, as they say in the song." I took another gulp of coffee and shook my head. "This is such a gift of time right now; I want to make some changes but I don't know where to start or what to do."

Nella listened carefully, and then she looked at me with a gleam in her eye and said: "Road trip! It was only a couple of days ago that you were telling me that you felt so free and at peace driving up the coast. You have your dad's car and enough money to cover gas and cheap accommodation. Take some time, focus on you."

I thought about it for a minute and smiled. "Yeah, yeah, I like that idea. I'll make it my *Recovery Road Trip*—my road trip to recover myself. I love it. And I'll have a mission on this trip. Last night, I had the most intense dream. I had been holding the little fig you gave me and thinking about the Divine Feminine before I went to sleep, so I think that must have impacted my dream. In my dream I met this woman, and she said that there was a secret to life. I'll never forget that—she said it so emphatically. I felt like everyone else knew this secret but I didn't. When I asked her what the secret was, she tilted her head and raised her eyebrow and said that I had to find out for myself. She looked so smug, I wanted to hit her, but instead I just started crying because I felt so frustrated that I had no idea what the secret was. And the woman just walked away while I was crying." I shook my head. "I woke up this morning feeling powerless and hopeless. So I will make it my mission to find out what other people know; I'll ask people along the way what their secret to life is. Maybe there is some giant secret that people know and that I can learn, or at least I can get a bit of clarity."

I sat back and looked intently at Nella. "So, Nells, what is your secret to life?"

Nella closed her eyes and thought about it for a few minutes. "I'm not sure I have a secret. I know that one of my absolute survival tactics is creativity. If I'm not creating something, I feel pretty low. I feel like creativity connects me to something bigger than me, if you know what I mean. But let me think, secret to life, hmmmmm. Um, maybe it would be something like 'love 'em anyway.'"

When I asked her what she meant, Nella explained that a lot of people in her life had let her down in various ways: financially, emotionally, physically. She continued: "And when I resented them for it, I always felt worse than before, always. I don't think many of them really cared one way or the other, but I always felt rotten. But then when I realized that I could love 'em anyway, despite their shortcomings, I always felt better. Mind you, I generally distanced myself from these people who let me down, but I didn't waste my energy resenting them and letting them take up space in my head. I sent them love, in that larger sense of the word, and then sent them on their way. So the love that I'm talking about is actually for me to feel better, not for the other person. I've been trying to live by that rule when I can."

I took a breath, feeling deep gratitude for the friendship that had sustained me for so many years. "You're a wise woman, Nella. Wise beyond your years."

"Let's get a map out and plan this road trip of yours. I'll make some more coffee, and we can play with this." Nella got up, got a new pot of coffee started, and went to get her big atlas.

"Where do you want to go?" she asked. She seemed almost as excited about the trip as I was.

"I want to go coast-to-coast," I said, looking at the map. "I'll drive from Seattle to Boston, across the whole country. But I don't want to just hurry directly across, I want to go to a few places from my past or places that I think will rejuvenate me. Let's see."

We looked at the big map of the US for a while and spent the next couple of hours mapping out a whole series of destinations. Some of the destinations were places I had been and wanted to revisit, like Missoula, Montana, Sun Valley, Idaho, and Madison, Wisconsin, but several others were places I had always wanted to go, but had never had the time, like Arches National Park, Utah and Ann Arbor, Michigan. Then there were others that I had never really wanted to go, but that fit in terms of driving time and distance, like Lincoln, Nebraska.

"I'll need to do a bit of research before I go to book some hostels or Airbnbs. Do you think I should book places for the whole trip now?"

"Well, it is July; it's probably a good idea to see what kind of accommodation is still available."

"Not only wise, but practical too. You will make someone a fine wife someday." I laughed.

Nella rolled her eyes. "Baby that ship has sailed. I am just fine on my own."

As we mapped out areas closer to Boston, there were still a couple of long days of driving, and I needed one more spot to stop. I searched the map for something to jump out at me on that route. "Oh, I've got it. Morgantown, West Virginia."

Nella laughed. "Of course, for the Joni Mitchell song."

And we both spontaneously started singing "Morning Morgantown" together, then dissolved into laughter.

By the end of our brainstorming session that afternoon, I felt a renewed sense of purpose and excitement. I wasn't sure exactly what I was going to find, but it felt like I was heading in the right direction.

When I got up two days later, the morning of my departure, Nella was sitting at the kitchen table waiting for me. In the middle of the table were two parcels wrapped in brown paper. Nella grinned: "One of my favorite things—packages wrapped in brown paper and tied up with string."

"Oh, Nells, what have you done?"

She smiled and handed me one of the packages. I opened it slowly. Inside was a CD with the title *Recovery Road Trip Playlist* written on it.

"Every good road trip needs a kick-ass playlist. After you went to bed, I stayed up and went through my old albums and CDs and made you a special playlist for your trip and put it on a CD. Do you have a CD player in that old Mustang? I didn't even think of that." I nodded and Nella continued. "I chose the songs for this playlist carefully;

9 — VICTIMHOOD

some of the songs for the route itself, many of the songs for our own history, and a lot of them just because I think they'll be good to listen to on the road. Actually, I had a blast making it."

"Oh, Nellie, that is so thoughtful! What is on it? I want to listen to it now."

"No, you have to wait til you're on the road, well out of Seattle and heading to Montana." She took a sip of coffee and then handed me the other parcel. "And this is for you to write about the secrets to life that you learn."

I opened the parcel to reveal a beautiful leather-bound journal. "Oh, Nell, this is gorgeous!"

"I actually bought it in Mexico last year but never found the time or energy to write in it. And that was because it was waiting for you. I love the idea that it will hold the secrets to life. Take meticulous notes and share it all with me when you get back here."

By this point, I had tears running down my cheeks, and my nose was running a bit as well. "Nells, you are amazing. I am so grateful that you are in my life."

"I love you too, my friend," she said as she handed me a tissue. "And I'll miss you—but this road trip feels like it has a life of its own now, and you better start moving."

"I know. That's what it feels like to me too. As much as I've loved licking my wounds and spending time healing here, I'm itching to get on the road."

"I'll meet you by the car," she said. "Just have to grab something!" With no further explanation, she dashed out of the kitchen toward her studio.

Shaking my head and smiling, I carried my bags out to my car. Just as I was closing my trunk, Nella came out to the driveway, carrying something small in her hands. She leaned into the car and placed it gently on the dashboard. Then she held out her hand. "Do you have your fig?"

"Of course I do!" I retrieved it from my pocket and handed it to her.

Tenderly, she put my little fig in the center of her creation. I sat in the driver's seat to take a closer look. Nella had made a small nest for the fig. She had woven a bit of straw, added some of her special feathers, and added a small flower or two. My little fig fit snugly in the center dip of the nest.

"I added just a wee bit of epoxy to the bottom to keep it from sliding around. And I gave it all a special blessing to protect you on the road."

I felt my heart swell. *Everyone should have a friend like Nella*, I told the universe silently.

I climbed back out of the car and looked at my friend, tears welling up in my eyes. "Oh God, Nells, I'm terrified."

Nella hugged me tightly. "Go live life large, my friend. And call me often so I can live vicariously through you. I love you."

We held each other for several minutes, and then I got into my car, started the engine, and waved as I backed out of the driveway on the first day of my journey.

## CHAPTER 2

*Love*

MISSOULA, MT

"*Love recognizes no barriers. It jumps hurdles, leaps fences,
penetrates walls to arrive at its destination full of hope.*"
—MAYA ANGELOU

J ust after passing through Spokane and into Idaho, I stopped at a
small diner and had a grilled cheese sandwich and an iced tea. I
planned to stop at as many old diners as possible. They reminded
me of places frozen in time. I felt safe there; when everything else was
changing faster than I could keep up, these places remained still. It
seemed like the décor was always the same, the Formica felt familiar,
and even the smells seemed the same, no matter what was on special.

As I sat at the scarred Formica table, I took a deep breath, trying
to shift the old heavy weight I was still carrying. Even though I had
been feeling excited to get on the road when I left Nella's, now that I
was away and alone in my head, I recognized the familiar knot in my
stomach and tight throat that let me know that fear and feelings of
alienation were taking over again. I thought of a quote by Janis Joplin:
"I'm a victim of my own insides." Spoken like a true addict.

I ate quickly and got back in my car, determined to shift my
mood. After greeting my little fig, I took Nella's playlist out—I had

promised her that I wouldn't put it on until I was well and truly out of Seattle, until I felt like I was really on the trip, and this felt like that time—and put it in the player.

I laughed out loud as the first song came on. An anthem from the seventies, Helen Reddy singing "I Am Woman." *Such an apt beginning, I thought, as I stretch my wings trying to relearn how to fly.* I thought back to when that song was popular and my whole life was ahead of me. I could almost touch that young woman, and I felt nostalgic for her.

I parked the car by the University of Montana so I could walk through the campus. As I strolled around the scenic campus, I recalled the last time I had been there. I had been about twenty years old, braless, barefoot, and high. It had been a crazy weekend, hanging out on campus, listening to music, and dancing like no one was watching.

I sat down on the grass near the clock tower and University Hall and closed my eyes. I could vividly see the tie-dyed T-shirt I had worn on that trip and could remember the acid I was tripping on at the time. I remember feeling confident in my body, like I could do anything—that I had my whole life ahead of me to be anything and go anywhere. I felt fearless. The sun was bright and warm, there weren't many people around, and I felt myself dozing off.

A Frisbee landed near me and woke me out of my nap. The sun was still relatively high, but the temperature was beginning to drop; the clock tower told me it was almost 6:00 p.m., so I had a quick Mexican dinner, found my Airbnb, and decided to give my friend Rosie a call in New Zealand.

On a cold midwinter afternoon, I figured Rosie would be in front of her fire at home. And I was right.

"Yay! I was hoping I'd hear from you soon," Rosie exclaimed as she answered the call.

"Are you home? Do you have time to talk?" I asked.

"Yes, of course I have time to talk to you. I'm just snuggled up by the fire reading the new book by Johann Hari. I'm all ears. Tell me what you've been up to. I haven't talked to you since the funeral."

"It's so good to hear your voice," I said as I put some hot water on to boil for tea. "I was just on the campus at the university here in Missoula, Montana. The last time I was here, I was about twenty years old."

"Let me guess—the last time you were there you were stoned out of your mind." She laughed. Rosie knew me so well. She and I had met in recovery in New Zealand, but she got sober several years before I got sober the first time and had stayed clean and sober, whereas I went out and used again for several years. I met Rosie on my return to recovery, about five years ago. I trusted her completely, for her compassion, wisdom, and love.

"Yep, you're right. I was remembering that young woman longingly as I wandered through the campus. I'm feeling pretty stuck to be honest. Feeling like life is passing me by and I'm just a bystander."

I filled my mug and dropped in a teabag, then sat in an armchair by the window in the living room.

"Sounds like you're stuck in a bit of victim consciousness," Rosie said. "What's up with that?"

"Yeah, that's what it feels like inside my head. Stuck, no way out, everything is beyond my control." My throat started to constrict. "I guess that's why I was remembering the young me so wistfully. That young woman was so footloose and free. She didn't feel stuck at all; the world was her oyster."

"You can remember her wistfully all you want, but don't make up stories that aren't true. You yourself have told me many a terrifying tale about what you got up to in your twenties. You're lucky you're alive. So don't whitewash a narrative about how grand it all was." That was Rosie, always cutting right to the truth.

I stood up and rolled my neck around. Although I appreciated my friend's ability to focus on the truth, it wasn't always easy to hear.

"But back up a minute, why are you in Montana of all places? You never mentioned anything about going there last time we talked."

I filled her in on my time at Nella's and my whole road trip plan. When I was done, she laughed and I heard her clap her hands together.

"Oh, I love it!" she exclaimed. "Are you going to go to meetings along the way to meet more people in recovery; is that part of this journey?"

"Yeah, that's definitely part of the plan. But it's also a journey to recover a part of me that I seem to have lost. So this recovery has a double meaning, if you know what I mean."

"Mmmm I get it. I like it. So do you have a plan or are you just meandering?"

"Oh, trust me, I've got a plan." I told Rosie about a few of the stops I had planned; she listened carefully, then interrupted about halfway through.

"Are you going to go to Boulder, Colorado by any chance?"

"Yes, in fact I am." I got up to get more tea while Rosie continued.

"Wonderful. I know a woman in recovery in Boulder. Her name is Rachel. I met her a few years ago at a meeting here in New Zealand. She's a sociology professor, specializing in addiction. A real switched-on woman. Remember that book by Johann Hari that I leant to you, *Chasing the Scream*? Well, she's the one that recommended it. You should look her up when you get to Boulder, I'm sure you two would hit it off."

I promised Rosie I would while trying to stifle a yawn.

"Oh, hon, you sound tired. I should let you go to bed; it's late there."

"Yeah, I am pretty exhausted. It's been a long day. But one more thing before we hang up, I want to tell you about a dream I had." I walked back to the armchair by the window and gazed outside while I described the dream in as much detail as I could remember; then I asked her if she had a life secret to share with me.

"Well, you know it's no secret. I talk about it all the time at meetings. It's about love, self-love. We gotta love ourselves and take care of ourselves. Until we learn to do that, nothing ever feels right. It's no mistake that on those chips we collect, it says: "To Thine Own Self Be True."

I smiled. No surprise, Rosie and Nella, two of the women I respected most, both thought that love was the secret.

After Rosie and I hung up, I sat by the window looking out at the millions of stars in the ink-black sky. It was not by chance that it was called "Big Sky Montana." I rolled my neck and shoulders a few more times to ease the stiffness. I contemplated having another cup of tea but knew I had already had too many and would no doubt be up several times to pee, so instead I went over to the bed, picked up my journal, and opened to the first page.

*Day One—Missoula Montana*

*Here I am in Missoula Montana; I've done it. I'm on my recovery road trip. I feel pretty damned proud of myself. I left Nella's place early this morning. I have an amazing mix tape that Nell made for me to keep me company, and this beautiful journal to write in every night. I plan to keep track of what I learn along the way. One of the goals on this trip is to ask people along the way about any special secrets to life that they have . . . starting today with the wisdom of my two dearest friends. As it turns out, both Nella and Rosie have the same idea . . . of course they do! They both believe that Love, in one form or another, is the secret to life; not like romantic love per se, but love in the biggest sense of the word, and certainly self-love. Rosie reminded me of the saying: "To thine own self be true." I'm going to keep that in mind on this trip.*

*And I read a wonderful quote by Dorothy Hunt today that really fits:*

> *In this choice-less, never-ending flow of life*
>
> *There is an infinite array of choices*
>
> *One alone brings happiness*
>
> *To love what is.*

*And so today I'm recording the first secret . . .*

*Secret #1*

*Love.*

## CHAPTER 3

# *Unity*

## SUN VALLEY, ID

*"Life doesn't make any sense without interdependence.
We need each other, and the sooner we learn that, the better for us all."*
—ERIK ERIKSON

I got up early, keen to get back on the road. I stroked my little fig statue in her nest; she had become my travel companion for the trip. I found myself talking to her often while driving and found a gentle solace knowing she was there. As I pulled out of Missoula, I told her about the first secret, musing aloud about love as I drove along Route 93. Ms. Fig was a great listener, and the scenery along the winding Bitterroot River was spectacular. As I meandered south, I stopped to watch some birds at a wildlife refuge; while they flew, I felt some of my own heaviness lift.

After hanging up with Rosie, the act of writing, of taking the stuff out of my head and getting it down on paper, proved to be a great sedative, and I found that I slept better that night than I had in weeks. At breakfast that morning, I had looked online for some 12-Step meetings in Ketchum. Rosie was right, I had been stuck in a victim mentality for several months and I was ready to move on. There were several meetings being held that night, and I was looking forward to attending a women's meeting where I could talk to fellow addicts about what was going on in my head. I was also hoping I could meet a few people to ask about their secrets to life.

When I got to Stanley, I felt like I was on a set for an old western movie. The town wasn't exactly as I had remembered it, but the scenery around it was just as magnificent as I had envisioned it. I found a pizzeria and ate the entire pizza with gusto. The sun was high and I wasn't in a hurry to get to Ketchum where I had booked a room for two nights, so I decided to drive down to Redfish Lake, where I'd camped many years earlier, to take a walk along the lake.

When I got down there, about twenty minutes later, the number of people by the lake surprised me. I remembered Redfish Lake as a quiet place, off the beaten track. But this was anything but that. There were motorboats zipping around, water skiers, and even a pontoon party boat. The snow-capped Sawtooth Mountains surrounding the lake were still glorious, but the busyness at the lake was not at all what I was in the mood for.

I found a large rock by the lake and sat down and lifted my face to the sun. I pulled out my phone, took a picture of the lake, and sent it to my sons. I left them a long audio telling them about Redfish Lake and musing about the fact that the last time I was there I was their age. It felt horribly uncomfortable to imagine my sons getting up to the same things that I did when I was last there. No mother wants to imagine their children taking drugs and having sex with random individuals. I shook my head to get rid of the image; it was way too jarring.

Ketchum had grown a lot since the last time I had been there. It felt a lot glitzier and fancier than when I lived there. Not a huge surprise since that was over thirty years ago. And since then, Bruce Willis and

Demi Moore had put the place on the map. It had always been a spot for celebrities, and from the look of it, the beautiful people had really taken over. But I was happy to see a few familiar buildings; The Pioneer Saloon and Whiskey Jacques still graced the main street. Of course it was the bars that I remembered best, drinking shots of tequila and swing dancing. It had been fun, but I also remembered waking up in strangers' homes wondering where I was; falling off my bike more than once trying to ride home after a drunken night out; the embarrassing stories that I heard about my behavior as I closed the bars down at the end of a rowdy night out. No I didn't need to be reminded by Rosie not to whitewash the narrative, I remembered the dark times too.

I wandered off the main street and meandered around until I found a cool-looking coffee shop. It had a nice vibe and I decided to have a fresh juice and enjoy the feel of the place. There was a woman sitting at a nearby table sipping a cup of tea and reading a book by Anne Lamott. Anyone reading anything by Annie Lamott was my kind of person. I wanted to talk to her but didn't want to interrupt her. I personally hate it when people interrupt me when I'm reading. I was looking at her, trying to decide what to do, when the woman looked up from her book and smiled at me. I felt so embarrassed to be caught staring at her, like I was spying on her. I went to pick up my juice and accidentally spilled it. I jumped up and narrowly avoided spilling it all over my lap as I moved out of the way.

"Oh dear," the woman said. She looked over at the counter and raised her voice, "Justin can you bring over a cloth; there's been a little spill. And maybe you could top up this poor woman's juice?"

I was mortified. "Oh God, how embarrassing!"

The guy behind the counter that had served me my juice just minutes before came over to my table with a wet cloth and a jug of juice. He wiped down the table and refilled the glass. "Do you need more tea, Stacy?"

"No, I'm good Justin, thanks."

Stacy looked over at me. "Do you want to join me at my table since yours is a bit wet at the moment?"

My heart was pounding, but I nodded. I had always been clumsy, especially when I was drinking, but I cringed at the thought that that might be someone's first impression of me. I was nervous and wanted this interesting-looking woman to like me; a common theme for me, wanting people to like me and often not feeling up to scratch. As I made my way over to her, I was extra careful about my footing.

"Hi, I'm Stacy; I work down the street at the library. I just locked up and needed a cup of tea. I haven't seen you before, so I'm guessing you're new to town. What brings you to Ketchum?"

"Hi, I'm Meg. Well, I used to live here many moons ago. I just buried my father and now I'm on a road trip to do some healing." I realized that this was probably too much information; I blushed and looked down. "Sorry, way too much information. I just keep embarrassing myself."

"Oh, please don't be embarrassed. Thank you for being so open. I miss that around here."

I looked up and smiled at her. I realized that Stacy was actually older than I first thought when I saw her. Her cool turquoise jewelry and colorful skirt caught my attention before the smile lines on her face. When I realized that Stacy was closer to my own age, I felt a bit less self-conscious.

"So when did you live here? I lived in Hailey for much of my youth, but I moved to New York as soon as I could. I couldn't wait to get out of here." She laughed a deep resonant laugh that made me smile. "And then after my divorce, I re-evaluated my life and wondered why I had left. I was working as a librarian in the city and realized I could work as a librarian anywhere and made my way back here."

I told Stacy about moving to New Zealand in my thirties and about coming back to the US for my dad's funeral. And then we both talked a bit about our childhoods, realizing we had a lot in common, both growing up in alcoholic families.

I grimaced when I told Stacey that the only places I remembered in Ketchum were the bars, and I told her a bit about my wild youth there.

"As a matter of fact," I disclosed, "I'm looking for a 12-Step meeting here in town."

"Oh there are plenty of those, believe me. We are a town of raging addicts or recovering addicts. Because of my own father's alcoholism, I chose to avoid booze, but I've gone to plenty of CoDA meetings, and one of my closest friends in town is in NA, I'll call her and find out if there's a good meeting today. Do you go to NA or do you only go to AA?"

"Oh, I go to either. My drug of choice was alcohol, but in my using days I wasn't choosy. My only preference is a meeting that focuses on emotional sobriety. I don't like pedantic Big Book thumping meetings. I've experienced way too many of those in my recovery. Now I steer clear of meetings that feel more judgmental than supportive."

Stacy laughed that deep laugh of hers and said: "Oh you are going to get along just fine with Melody." She took out her phone, called her friend, and told her that I was looking for a meeting. "She said she doesn't like, quote, 'pedantic Big Book thumping meetings' unquote." Stacy listened and started laughing. "Yeah, I figured she would be your kinda woman." Then she took a pencil and an old receipt out of her purse and wrote something down. "Hey, Mel, what are you doing tomorrow night? How about dinner at my place?" Stacy took the phone away from her face and looked at me. "Are you still around tomorrow night?" I nodded. "Great. Want to come over for a barbecue? Nothing fancy, just having a meal together while you're in town."

I smiled and nodded. "I would love that, thank you."

Stacy put the phone back up to her mouth, "OK, great, Meg can come too. Let's meet at my place about six thirty. See you tomorrow."

Stacy put her phone back in her purse, wrote something else on the receipt, and then handed it to me. "Here's the info about the meeting. And I wrote my address just below that for the barbecue tomorrow."

"Oh God, you are so kind. Thank you for this. And let me bring something to dinner tomorrow. I don't have a kitchen at the place I'm staying, but I could pick up something for dessert. How about some strawberries and ice cream?"

"That would be wonderful. Thanks. Well, I've got to get home. It's been lovely to meet you Meg, and I'm looking forward to getting to know you better tomorrow night."

"Me too, Stacy, see you then."


As I approached the NA meeting building an hour later, I noticed a woman standing alone near the entrance looking at her phone. I walked up to her and introduced myself.

"Hi, I'm Meg, are you Melody?"

"Yes, hi, welcome." At first Melody put out her hand to shake hands, then thought better of it and wrapped me in a hug. "Come on in, this meeting usually is pretty good about starting on time. It's a small women's meeting, intimate and real. I loved the fact that you told Stace that you don't like pedantic meetings. I cannot bear half the meetings in town for just that reason. But this one is very real. A lot of emotional sobriety in this room." I felt some tension leave my body; it sounded exactly like the kind of meeting I had been hoping to find.

As we walked in, it took a moment for my eyes to adjust. The room was dim, with several comfortable-looking chairs arranged in a circle. There were already eight women sitting in the circle chatting. There was a tureen of hot water and several different tea selections on a table against the wall.

"Hi, Mel," a woman called out. "Grab some tea for yourself and your friend, and we'll get started."

Melody and I walked over to the table. "What would you like?" Melody asked. "I'm having peach; it's a good one."

"That sounds wonderful, thanks," I answered as I looked around the room. It looked like some kind of community center meeting room; there were toys in one corner and posters from different community groups up on the walls. On a table near the group sat a small vase of wildflowers and a lit candle.

Melody handed me my tea and said: "Let's find a seat." We sat down; I took a deep breath, closed my eyes, and felt myself melt a bit into the soft armchair. I felt safe and at home.

The woman who had greeted us opened the meeting: "Hi, everybody. I'm April, and I'm an addict, and I'll be your chairperson tonight."

Everyone responded: "Hi, April."

"Let's open this meeting with a moment of silence, followed by the Serenity Prayer."

After the women recited the Serenity Prayer, April continued.

"Are there any newcomers or guests?"

I raised my hand and introduced myself, and the group greeted me, then April spoke to the group.

"Tonight I'd like to talk about Tradition One: *Our common welfare should come first; personal recovery depends on NA unity.* The reason I want to talk about that is because I went to a really shitty meeting in Twin Falls yesterday, and I thought I better talk about it to some people in recovery who understand what I'm talking about and can help me get past it."

April took a big breath and continued. "It was an AA meeting, and there were a lot of old-timers there. I introduced myself as an addict, and one of the men said, 'This is an AA meeting' and glared at me. During the rest of the meeting, I felt like a pariah. I need to talk about it so that my resentment and frustration with that closed mentality doesn't fester. And I know my recovery depends on our unity, so tonight I need to hear from all of you about how you practice unity, especially in the face of the divisiveness that seems to be everywhere these days, not only in these rooms. Thanks."

"Thanks, April," the women murmured. Everyone in the room shared about their yearning for connection, how the unconditional support of people in the rooms helped them stay clean and sober, and each woman shared at least one story similar to April's, where the judgement and lack of acceptance kept them from certain meetings. Finally April looked at me and said: "Meg, would you like to share?"

I took a breath and looked at the women in the circle. "Hi, I'm Meg and I'm an addict. Thanks so much for welcoming me in this powerful circle of recovering women. This meeting is exactly what I needed today." I briefly told the story of going home to bury my alcoholic father, of the recovery road trip, and of my quest to find out the secret to life. "And tonight I really hear that one of those secrets must be unity. I was clean and sober for a while, and because of meetings and people just like all of you have been describing, I decided to quit going to meetings. I just didn't feel the unity anymore. And when I quit going to meetings, it wasn't long before I decided that I could drink again. It took me several years drinking again before I found my way back to recovery. So it's really true that my personal recovery depends on our unity. I can't forget that."


After the meeting, a few women went out for tea at a small café near there. I decided that it was the perfect opportunity to ask my question, given that I had a captive audience.

I cleared my throat. "Is it OK if I ask you all a question?" When they all nodded, I described my quest to try to understand my dream and find out if other people knew a secret to life that I had been missing.

When I was done explaining and had posed my question, a couple of the women laughed good naturedly, and there were a few jokes, but most of the women were intrigued and the table grew quiet.

Dee, a middle-aged schoolteacher said: "I haven't really thought about it in that way, but I guess that freedom would be my secret to a good life."

And Sandy, a retired firefighter, said: "I think the most important thing is one's health; being healthy and feeling safe makes for a good life for me."

I took my notebook out of my backpack. "Do you all mind if I take a few notes while you're talking?"

April, the woman who chaired the meeting smiled and said: "No I don't mind at all. Anyone else?" They all shook their heads.

"I've been thinking a lot about what we talked about tonight," April said. "So maybe unity is the secret to a good life. I think of unity as being together or at one with someone or something. It's the opposite of being divided. To me, it's all about connection."

Melody nodded as April spoke. "Yeah, I agree. I mean it may not be my secret to a wonderful life, but I do believe it's essential to a good life anyway. I think unity brings us tolerance, receptivity, and oneness; to me it describes an openness, a curiosity instead of a closed-mindedness. There is so much divisiveness in this country and all over the world right now that I just need to believe we all really can connect."

Everything that Melody and April had shared really resonated with me. There was a calmness that settled in my stomach, a rightness about the whole concept of unity and connection.

As I walked back to my studio, I paused often to look up, marveling at the jagged mountains touching the sky and the millions of stars above me. Before I got into bed, I made a few more notes in my little notebook, things to add to my journal later, and fell asleep thinking about the cool women I had spent the evening with, grateful for the connections. I had been learning the hard way that what I needed in 12-Step meetings was real connection and support. I had thought that all meetings would offer that, but I was wrong. I had been to too many meetings where I was told to shut up and listen, not talk about my feelings, just don't pick up a drink and I'd be fine. But I wasn't. I was left feeling frustrated, empty, and unseen. That was one of the main reasons I hadn't stayed in recovery, because I didn't feel that camaraderie and support. But now, my second time around, I had learned to look for meetings where I felt at home and connected to the other recovering people.

The day dawned bright and sunny, and I was excited to get going. I asked the woman at the Airbnb if I could borrow a bike to ride into Sun Valley. Riding out, my first stop was the coffee shop where I had met Stacy. I got a coffee and a delicious cinnamon roll. Feeling charged up on sugar and caffeine, I easily biked the fifteen-minute ride. As I explored the resort and looked around, it felt familiar, but very different. After riding around for about an hour, I got a coffee, sat by the ice rink, and watched the skaters for a while. I watched a couple of young girls getting lessons on the ice, remembering the numerous times I had skated at that same ice rink. I remembered feeling so self-conscious back then, not a good enough skater, not at all like the other girls skating in groups. My parents wanted me to take lessons, so I did, but I hated it. I didn't fit in on the ice or with the skaters, a familiar feeling when I was young, not fitting in with the cool kids.

I got back on my bike and rode around the periphery of the resort. The smell of sagebrush brought with it a longing; I remembered riding a friend's horse there. I was much more comfortable on the back of a horse than in a skirt on the ice. I had told my parents that I wanted to ride horses, not ice-skate. But they forbade that and said it wasn't ladylike. I wished that I had had the courage to stand up for myself back then instead of always trying to please my parents. I wondered if I had stood up to them then if it would have alleviated some of that stuckness now.

At six, I walked to the supermarket and bought ice cream, strawberries, and a small bouquet of flowers for Stacy, then walked the four short blocks to Stacy's house.

I found Stacy and Melody sitting on the front porch on an old-fashioned swing, having a cup of iced tea. They both waved as I walked up the pebbled path. We moved to the back deck where the barbecue was warming up.

Stacy got me a glass and poured some iced tea; the chicken sizzled as it was placed on the grill, and the aroma was enticing.

"So, Meg, how's it all going? Melody told me you made it to the meeting," Stacy said as she sat down. Then she paused and looked at Melody. "It's OK that we talked about that right? I mean anonymity and all that?"

Melody smiled. "It's fine." She looked at me and quickly said, "I didn't disclose any personal details, of course."

I laughed: "Oh God, I don't care at all. Actually, Stacy, it was a wonderful group of women, and I'm so grateful that you directed me there. Plus, I had the opportunity to ask my life secret question."

Stacy looked at me with a puzzled expression: "What question is that?"

My cheeks colored. "Oh wow, I thought I had told you at the café when I met you. I blathered on about so much of my history, I thought I had told you about my dream and my question too." I looked down and sipped my iced tea, a tightness in my stomach telling me that I had somehow screwed up.

"No, you didn't, but it sounds interesting, go on." Stacy made a motion with her hands for me to continue.

Immediately, I felt better. With a smile, I described my dream and told her that finding out about people's secret to life had become an essential part of this journey.

"Sort of a *Quest Question*," Melody added with a grin.

"Yes, that's it; it is my Quest Question." I put down my tea and looked at Stacy. "So, what's your secret to life? The topic of last night's meeting was unity, so a lot of women discussed that as one possible answer."

Stacy listened closely, then closed her eyes and quoted Gwendolyn Brooks: "We are each other's harvest; we are each other's business; we are each other's magnitude and bond."

She paused and then added: "I like the idea of unity, but also of, let's see, I guess solidarity would be the word; unity in the spiritual sense, solidarity in the practical sense. I like the image of us standing shoulder to shoulder. I'm an activist from way back. I like to see myself in solidarity with others fighting for the underdog. I think that gives my life meaning."

I rummaged through my backpack for my notebook and a pen. "Thank you, Stacy, I like how you worded that."

I wrote it down before I could forget.


After we finished eating, we went into Stacy's house to do the dishes. As we worked, Stacy and Melody asked me about New Zealand. I described the town where I lived and the beach near my house. They both agreed that they'd love to visit one day.

As I was getting ready to leave, Stacy went to her bookcase and grabbed a book to give me. "Here, Meg. I think that this book will really help with your Quest Question." She handed me a book that Rosie had talked about but that I had not read yet, *Life Visioning* by Michael Bernard Beckwith.

I was touched. "Wow, Stacy, thank you so much. I've actually wanted to read this for a while. A friend of mine in New Zealand talked to me about this book last year. But are you sure you won't miss it? I mean, I'll mail it back to you when I finish."

"No, it's fine, I've read it. Maybe I'll pick it up from you in New Zealand one day."

"That sounds perfect."

I hugged Stacy and Melody goodbye and headed back to my studio in the chilly mountain air, my heart full.

Back inside, I turned on the heat and made a cup of chamomile tea and then sat at the small desk to write.

*Day Two and Three—Ketchum and Sun Valley Idaho*

*What a surprising couple of days this has been. I didn't anticipate the range of emotions that coming back here would bring up. On a bike ride today around Sun Valley, I had so many flashbacks and visceral memories. It evoked so many feelings of powerlessness from when I was a kid, being told to be something that I absolutely wasn't, and told not to be who I really was. It's so eye opening. All of my people-pleasing and denying what I want and even who I really am, going all the way back to when I was young, have really contributed to my feelings of alienation and how stuck I feel now.*

*On a brighter note, I didn't figure on making new friends on this journey. I thought I would be pretty isolated and keep to myself most of the time. But I have met two women that I believe I will stay in touch with and may even come visit me one day. These two strangers have been so warm and welcoming and kind. Reinforcing the message that I need connection. After dinner tonight, Stacy gave me a copy of a book that Rosie told me about last year that I've been meaning to read, Life Visioning by Michael Bernard Beckwith. It felt so serendipitous.*

*At both the meeting and the conversation tonight, we ended up talking about unity. It all just feels so connected and so meant to be. Connection and Unity . . .*

*So I've decided . . .*

*Secret #2*

*Unity.*

# The Thoughts We Choose

ARCHES NATIONAL PARK, UT

CHAPTER 4

---

*"The thoughts we choose to think*
*are the tools we use to paint the canvas of our lives."*
—LOUISE L. HAY

I drove out of Ketchum early the next morning with some sadness. It had been a great stop. I had made two new friends and confirmed that connection was a real key to my recovery.

After about four and a half hours on the road, I got to Salt Lake City, where I decided to stop for lunch. I had heard that Salt Lake City was known for its burgers, so I stopped at a place recommended online, and man, I was not disappointed. My burger, topped with pastrami and cheese and accompanied by French fries, was heavenly.

After the enormous meal, I really needed to walk for a while, so I took my time exploring Temple Square. The centerpiece, of course, was the enormous Mormon Temple. The ornate spires and flowers of orange, red, and yellow in the surrounding gardens were beautiful. It was hot in the sun, but I was reluctant to leave, not knowing if I'd ever be there again. I thought about taking a tour, but in the end decided against it due to the hordes of people with the same idea.

By two thirty, I was back in the car headed for Moab. The route I took was a two-lane road through a narrow canyon; the red rocks were interesting but driving on the small road required full focus to stay on the road and avoid the potholes; I felt my shoulders tighten and my body tense as I leaned closer to the steering wheel.

By the time I finally arrived in Moab just after 7:00 p.m., I felt the beginning of a headache coming on.


Moab, the gateway to Arches National Park, was a colorful, picturesque town surrounded by twisted and worn sandstone shaped by Mother Nature's own hands. It had the very distinct feel of an international outdoor playground for extreme sports enthusiasts. The people wandering the streets looked fit and healthy, ready to climb, ride, and explore, like they just stepped off a billboard advertising clean living. I felt distinctly old, frumpy, and out of shape as I slowly walked along the sidewalk in my loose crumpled shorts and tee shirt. I regretted my lunch choice as it sloshed around in my belly.

While I was checking into the hostel, I noticed a big sign on the wall: "'If it is to be, it is up to me'—William Johnsen"

I took a picture to remind me of it and thought, *Yeah, that's going to be my new motto. No more feeling like a victim, no more feeling like life is passing me by.* But the youthful, sporty vibe of the town did not match my mood. I felt decidedly middle-aged and out of shape. With lunch like ballast in my belly and my body stiff after the long drive, I was tired and cranky and did not want to interact with anyone, so I decided to skip dinner and turn in early.

On the single bed in my small musty room, I started the book that Stacy had given me. In the book, Beckwith wrote about evolving through stages. The whole process of evolving that was described in the book, zigzagging, with ups and downs, felt sort of like my road trip. I came to the realization that my hoped-for shift in consciousness was not going to be a direct journey. In "Stage One—Victim Consciousness," the idea that "Life happened *to* me" felt accurate; it felt like I had lived in that stage for quite a while. But I thought back to the sign in the office, if I was going to change and move beyond that, then it was up to me.

I jumped ahead to read about "Stage Two—Manifestor Consciousness." "Yes," I said out loud, "I am the driver of my life. Life happens *by* me. I will make my life happen." I took the small notebook out of my bag and wrote some notes:

*As I evolve from victimhood, I release blame, shame, and guilt. I feel powerful.* And below that I wrote the quote from the office: "*If it is to be, it is up to me.*"

The next morning, I listened to a meditation that Rosie had sent me. Her email had a quote by Deepak Chopra: "We understand that the source of power is not outside of us. It is within us."

After the meditation, I felt a renewed conviction and went out to find some breakfast. I found a small café where I ordered some muesli and coffee. But, as I sipped my coffee and looked around, it was clear that I didn't belong here. I considered just packing up my car and heading back to Seattle, but I figured I might as well see the park since I was already there, so I got in my car and began the short drive to the entrance to the park.

I once did a report on Arches National Park when I was in seventh or eighth grade, and I remembered reading that it was a "red rock wonderland." The pictures in the encyclopedia from the library at school made it look like another planet—a landscape of reds and ochre with soaring pinnacles, stacked boulders, and giant balanced rocks. I remember feeling so inspired and thought of it as a place that I could escape to one day.

But on the short drive to the park, I knew that this was not my "escape place." It was already hot as I approached the entrance, and the line of cars waiting to get into the park confirmed that my timing was way off. I had not counted on the crowds. I had imagined the vast landscapes that I had seen in pictures, empty and open. As I drove into the line and waited, people biked and walked past the car, the sun rose higher, and the day grew hotter. I knew I was going to be in line for at least an hour.

When I finally entered the park, I gaped at the red rocks creating a Mars-like terrain, but the interesting yellow arches just served to frame the hundreds of people snapping pictures of the formations. The shine had worn off with the wait to get in, the number of people, and the heat. I wandered around a bit, but there was not much shade, and I felt hot and bothered. I really tried to capture that awe that I had felt as an adolescent when I did the report, but I just couldn't get there. I was so disappointed and frustrated. I half-heartedly took a few pictures, but they were mostly washed out, not matching at all the majestic splendor of my memory. I deleted most of the pictures and slowly walked back to my car, feeling dejected. I realized that I had spent more time in the car waiting to get into the park than I did walking around inside. I just wanted to get back to my room, stand under a cool shower, and take a nap.


By the time I woke up, the sun was going down and the temperature had dropped down to a tolerable level. I thought about going back to the park to watch the sunset, but I just could not muster any enthusiasm. I found myself thinking about returning to Seattle, and questioning whether the whole trip was a good idea after all.

I looked online for restaurant recommendations and decided that Mexican food would help shift my mood. There was a small Mexican restaurant a short walk from my hostel.

I walked over only to be told that there was an hour's wait for a table. "Shit, typical," I muttered as I walked away.

———

Instead of green enchiladas for dinner, I went to a small grocery store and bought some bread, cheese, and a bottle of water; I walked to a park, sat on the grass in some shade, and ate the meager meal—but I was still hungry when I finished, so I went back to the store and bought a tub of rocky road ice cream.

I walked slowly back to the hostel, shoulders slumped and feet kicking up dust. There were some young people sitting outside at a picnic table drinking beer, playing guitar, singing and laughing. I hated all of them. I glared at one young woman with long tan legs and blond braids playing hacky sack, but when she looked up innocently and smiled at me, I felt ridiculous and hurried back to my hostel.

Back in my room, I sat alone, feeling miserable, eating the ice cream and watching dumb videos. "What was I thinking, taking this journey?" I said to myself. "I'm too old and set in my ways for this. This was such a mistake."

I finished the entire tub of ice cream and felt bloated and nauseous by the end of it. I took another cool shower and lay down on the bed; I thought about reading some more of the Beckwith book, but I just could not muster the energy. I reluctantly pulled out my journal.

*Days Four and Five—Moab Utah*

*I don't feel like writing anything. I'm in a shitty mood and I don't want to do this anymore. I am too old and unfit. This place is very pretty in a lot of ways, but I don't feel like I belong here at all. I don't know why I decided to do this in the first place. What is the point? I just feel blah . . . and the tub of ice cream I just consumed did not help.*

*Secret . . . ? I didn't get a secret from anyone, but I saw a sign . . .*

*"If it is to be, then it is up to me" . . . is that a life secret? Not sure. But if it's all up to me, I'm in serious trouble . . .*

## CHAPTER 5

# *Compassion*

## THE GRAND CANYON, AZ

---

*"We must accept finite disappointment, but never lose infinite hope."*
—DR. MARTIN LUTHER KING, JR.

I woke up with shame coiling in my stomach like a snake. Eating a tub of ice cream wasn't as bad as waking up with a hangover after a blackout, but I still felt wretched. I quietly packed up the room and surreptitiously threw away the tub on the way out, as if anyone besides me would care that I ate the ice cream.

As I left Moab, the sun was rising. I had learned an important lesson about the heat in the Southwest: avoid it if at all possible. I knew the drive to Flagstaff was over five hours, and I wanted to be able to wait out the heat of the day at the hostel before I drove to the South Rim of the Grand Canyon for the sunset. I was determined not to make the same mistakes I had made at Arches. I would miss the heat and skip all the junk food.

The woman at the hostel that I had spoken to the day before advised me to drive through Monument Valley, that it was not to be missed. Along the road, long sandstone fingers in hues of burnt umber and sienna reached toward the sky, but driving felt so treacherous that I could barely take my eyes off the road directly in front of me to enjoy the scenery. The numerous potholes and switchbacks were more than I had counted on. Once again, my focus on the road was causing my body to tense up, and I could feel a dull ache starting at the base of my skull. I wished I had a companion to share the experience and give me a break. I looked briefly at Ms. Fig and told her that I wished she could share the driving, but she didn't answer.

By the time I drove into Flagstaff, my shoulders felt like there was an iron bar running through them. Not even the music could lift my mood, and just as I started to relax a bit at the thought of a hot shower, I heard and felt a dull thump, thump, thump. "Oh, fucking perfect," I screamed. "A flat tire, exactly what I was hoping for today."

I pulled over and looked at the tire. It was indeed flat, not that I needed confirmation. I opened the trunk and looked for the jack and the spare. I finally located what I thought was the jack, but I wasn't even sure how to put it together, and the spare was bald and would not be safe to drive on. I felt miserable, utterly defeated.

I slid down the car and put my head against the door. I felt the sweat trickle down my forehead as I sat in the full sun on the dry, cracked dirt on the side of the road. I put my head in my hands and just sobbed. All the driving and time alone had given me plenty of time to think. I wasn't sure if this was a full existential crisis, but it was close. My job paid the bills but didn't give me a lot of fulfillment; I had no partner; my kids were grown and doing fine on their own; there was no one who really needed me. What was the point to it all? Was there even a point, or was this it?

A red ant bit me on the thigh and drove me back to my feet. I got back in the car and drove slowly into town.

———

The mustang limped into a small service station at the edge of town. A burly man with a beer gut walked out of the garage, wiping his hands on an oily rag. I turned off the engine and got out of the car.

"Looks like you got yourself a flat tire there, missy," the man said with a lascivious grin, looking me up and down.

I felt dirty watching him undress me with his eyes. Being alone in a new town with a creep eyeing me increased my already high level of anxiety and left my breathing shallow and my stomach in a knot.

I took a deep breath and replied as breezily as I could manage, "Yes, obviously. I'm hoping you can fix it. Hold on a second, I promised I'd check in with my friend as soon as I got to town. She's expecting me." I pulled out my phone and called Nella. Nella answered on the first ring as though she had been waiting for my call.

"Yay, I was hoping I'd hear from you," Nella exclaimed.

"Hi, Nella, I'm here. I should be at your house really soon," I said loudly, then turned my back to the man and walked out of earshot and spoke in a low voice. "Just stay on the line with me OK. I don't feel safe right now."

"Oh shit! What's going on? Tell me what's happening," Nella said.

"I will in a minute. Just please stay on the line." I turned around and walked back toward the car and continued my made-up conversation with Nella. "Yes, it was a great drive, but I have a flat tire. Hold on, OK?" I looked at the guy and gave him my most self-assured look. "Do you have the size tire I need for the car?"

The man walked over to the car and looked at the size on the tire. "Uh, yep, I do. But you'll have to wait til I finish with the truck I'm working on. It'll be at least an hour. You can wait right over there in my office," he said and had the audacity to wink at me.

I imagined his office, full of girly pictures on the wall and said: "No, thanks. I have a friend waiting for me in town."

"Suit yourself," he said as he shrugged and turned his head to spit out a wad of chewing tobacco as he walked away.

"Wait," I said. "About how much will it cost?"

"Oh, round about 150 to 170 dollars when it's all done." He continued walking toward the garage. "I'll try to get to it after I finish up with the truck. You can go into the office there and grab yourself a card so you have the number. Call me at about three thirty."

I took a deep breath and put the phone back up to my ear and said in a chirpy voice: "So anyway, I'm in town and I'll be at your house soon. Can't wait to see you."

"What's going on Meg? Where are you?" Nella asked anxiously.

"I'm just getting a card in the office of the garage on the edge of town; you probably know it. It's called, uh . . ." I looked up at the sign on the garage. "Billy Joe's. It's not far from you. I'm walking over now," I said like everything was fine, and then I lowered my voice: "Hold on, Nell, I'll explain everything in a minute."

I went back to my car, took the car key off the ring, and took my backpack out of the back seat, and then I walked into the office and looked around. There were no girly pics, but the stains on the wall and saggy couch, plus the burnt-out light bulb, made me want to rush out of there. I put the key on the counter, grabbed a card, and hurried out. As I passed the man, he grunted a goodbye but didn't lift his head from inside the engine of the truck he was working on.

I started walking toward town and lifted the phone back up to my ear. "Are you still there, Nella?"

"Of course I'm still here. Now what the hell is going on, Meg? Are you OK? Where are you?"

"Yeah, yeah, I'm fine." I felt my throat tightening up and could feel tears that I had managed to push down in the garage resurface. "I'm in Flagstaff, Arizona. I got a flat tire, and I couldn't change it, and the mechanic gave me the creeps; he was leering at me and I felt so vulnerable all alone, so I called you and pretended I had a friend in town and was headed to your house so he didn't think I was on my own. I'm so fucking pathetic."

"Oh, Megs. It sounds horrible, but you're OK? You're not hurt or in trouble?" Nella asked, sounding less frightened, but still concerned.

"Yeah, I'm OK. Sorry to freak you out like that." My throat continued to constrict; it felt like someone had stuck a rag in it. "Oh, Nells, what am I doing? What am I trying to prove? Can I just come back to your house?" I spotted a bench under a tree at a small park across the road and walked over and sat down. "I can't do this. I didn't even know how to change the damn tire. I've had plenty of time to think while driving, and I really don't know why I'm even doing this trip. I don't belong here; I'm sitting on this bench in a little park and watching all these young people here; everyone is on mountain bikes and skateboards. They're all so damn sporty and young; they all look like they are about to abseil down into the canyon and ride the rapids on the river. And all I'm doing is eating tubs of ice cream alone." I swiped my wet cheeks with the back of my hand.

"Oh, honey. It sounds like you've had a tough day. I wish I really did live there so you could come over," Nella said softly. "But for now, are you far from your accommodation? Can you walk there from where you are?"

"Hold on, I'll look."

I took the phone from my ear and looked up how far I was from the hostel. "Yeah, I can walk, it's not far."

"OK then, what I want you to do is get to wherever you are staying so you have a bit of space. Maybe take a shower, or at least splash your face, and then call me back so we can talk. OK?"

"OK, yeah I can do that. I'll call you back soon."


As I walked by a small shop on the way to the hostel, I realized that I hadn't eaten much all day. I bought some crackers and cheese, then walked to the hostel and went up to my room. The room was dingy, but it had a bathroom, and it was private. I took a long shower and tried to loosen the knot in my stomach and the cramp in my shoulders. Then I sat down at the foot of the bed to eat and called Nella back.

Nella answered on the first ring again. "Hi, Megs. How are you feeling now?"

"Better after a shower and a bit of food. Excuse me for crunching in your ear, but I realized I haven't eaten much today, a reaction after overeating yesterday."

"So start from the beginning and tell me what's happened since you left Seattle."

"Um, let me see, how many days ago was that? I was in Missoula, a couple of days in Sun Valley, then Moab and the drive today. Wow, it's been less than a week. I feel like I've been gone for ages."

"Yeah, you left six days ago. I've been watching your progress on that map we made before you left."

I closed my eyes and fell back against the pillows, looking up at the ceiling, "Jeez, it's been a long day. But Nells, I meant what I said; can I come home? Please?"

"Of course you can, you can come back here whenever you want to. But tell me what's brought this on? What happened?"

"It all just feels too hard, and I feel too old to be doing this. I just don't feel up to all this; I didn't plan things well yesterday, I got out late, it was hot, and there were thousands of people there, and I already told you about today. Shit, Nella, I really feel like I just can't do anything right." I sat up. "Oh God, I just remembered, I never thanked you for the playlist CD. I love it. It has been my companion and a godsend on this trip. And I find myself talking to my little nested fig several times a day; she has absolutely become my sacred traveling companion. I'm so sorry I didn't thank you before now."

"I'm so glad you like the music and the fig, and so glad they've kept you company. That is really good to hear."

I got up and looked out the small window in the room, which unfortunately had a view of the brick wall next door. The curtains were torn and dirty, and the carpet wasn't much better. "God, this room is dismal. But I feel better being able to share it all with you."

"Well, good. Then call me more often."

"I promise I will." I bit off a chunk of cheese and swallowed. "Thanks for being there, Nells."

"Of course, anytime. But let me say, there are going to be ups and downs; you've undertaken a huge journey, Megs. I mean, honestly, I don't know many women our age that would have the courage to do what you are doing. You are amazing. I mean that."

"Thanks, Nell. On my better days, I do feel proud of myself for doing this."

"Before you go, I want to tell you about a podcast I listened to by a woman named Kristin Neff. It was a wonderful talk about self-compassion. I'll email you the link; I think you would like it. It feels very timely."

"Oh, I'd love that, thanks." I looked up at the naked bulb. "I need some motivation and inspiration at the moment."

"This reminds me of a quote by Martin Luther King: 'We must accept finite disappointment, but never lose infinite hope.'"

"Thanks, Nells. You're my saving grace. I love you, my friend."

"I love you back. Take some pics of the sunset tonight and call me more often, promise?"

"Will do."

I dialed the number on the card for Billy Joe the mechanic at three thirty, as instructed. He assured me that the car would be ready in the next fifteen minutes. Then I called the Airbnb in Taos to find out if I could come a day early. I was relieved when the woman at the other end of the phone said that I was in luck and the room was available. I had planned to stay in Flagstaff for two days to do some hiking, but between the depressing room and vibe of the town, I just wanted to get out. I would drive to the rim, watch the sunset over the canyon, and then leave in the morning.

I hoped I wasn't making a mistake. I didn't know if I would ever be back here again and didn't want to regret not staying longer. But when I walked out of the hostel and was almost run down by a couple of teenage boys skateboarding on the sidewalk, I decided that I had made the right decision.

When I got back to Billy Joe's, my car was parked in front of the shop with a new tire on it. I walked into the office and pulled out my credit card.

"That'll be 200 dollars," Billy Joe said as he handed me the invoice and key. I noticed he had a new wad of chewing tobacco bulging out of his bottom lip.

I winced. "What? I thought you said it would cost between 150 and 170 dollars."

"Well, tires for these old Mustangs are a specialty item, missy."

I had no idea if that was true or not, and I was frustrated that I was powerless in the situation and couldn't argue the point. I sighed and handed him my credit card and waited for the receipt. He gave me the receipt and a horrible, tobaccoey grin.

"Here you go. You travel safe now." He chuckled as I turned to leave. I could feel his eyes on me as I walked out the door.

*Yuck. You old pig*, I thought as I left. I wished I had the courage to call him on his behavior, but I felt too vulnerable and alone.

As I'd feared, there were hundreds of tourists at the South Rim when I got there that evening, and most of them seemed to have state of the art cameras and tripods. Armed with only my phone's camera, I felt the familiar twist in the pit of my stomach of not being good enough and not being well prepared. But even with the crowds of people and the lack of a decent camera, the slowly descending sun and emerging colors confirmed my choice to be there. The majesty of the changing colors in both the sky and the canyon itself: the indigo, magenta, and orange of the sky, and the reds, yellows, and browns of the canyon was a spectacle not to be missed. As I watched the sunset, I was reminded of the quote that Nella had shared, and I decided that I could not lose infinite hope.

By the time I got back to the hostel that night, it was after ten o'clock. I took a quick shower and got into bed, then clicked on the link that Nella had sent and watched as Kristin Neff explained the three components of self-compassion.

The more I listened, the softer I felt toward myself.

Before I went to sleep, I took out my journal and began to write.

*Day Six—Flagstaff, Arizona, and The Grand Canyon*

*I've been feeling like shit, so lonely and just bad at doing life; I honestly cannot remember why I'm even doing this trip. It just feels hard. What is the point? I'm seriously thinking about heading back to Seattle . . . but for the moment, I'll keep heading east, one day at a time.*

*When I was talking to Nella, she recommended a TED Talk to watch online. It was by a woman named Kristin Neff, an expert on self-compassion. It was so wonderful to listen to Neff speak. I need to buy her book for sure. I learned about three elements of self-compassion:*

*1. Self-kindness vs. Self-judgment.*

*2. Common humanity vs. Isolation.*

*3. Mindfulness vs. Over-identification.*

*All three feel very relevant to me at the moment. In terms of self-kindness, Neff explained that self-compassion means being understanding toward myself when I fuck up instead of beating myself up mercilessly; that I don't have to be so self-*

*critical and angry at myself all the time when I don't do "it" (whatever it is) right.*

*In terms of common humanity, I'm not the only person in the world that doesn't have it all together, that there is a shared experience, something we all go through, that it's not just me alone failing.*

*And self-compassion encourages me not to over focus on me, to learn to put my own situation into a bigger perspective, learn to be more mindful and nonjudgmental—to not deny my feelings but not wallow in them either. This is so helpful.*

*One sentence in the talk stood out for me: "If you are continually judging and criticizing yourself while trying to be kind to others, you are drawing artificial boundaries and distinctions that only lead to feelings of separation and isolation." That really resonates. I'm constantly judging and criticizing myself. I hold myself to a different standard than I hold others, and I end up feeling separate and isolated. And it sucks. It all ties together, thinking back to my realization in Sun Valley—my people-pleasing and self-denial leaves me feeling alienated and stuck.*

*I am committed to being kinder to myself. I will be more mindful of how I speak to myself and treat myself. So after talking to Nella and watching Neff talk, I have decided:*

*Secret #3*

*Compassion—especially self-compassion.*

## CHAPTER 6

*Kindness*

TAOS, NM

> *"Always be a little kinder than necessary."*
> —JAMES M. BARRIE

I t was just after 6:00 a.m. when I woke up; the room was stuffy and warm. I could tell it was going to be another hot day. I stretched and planned on getting an early start. Before jumping out of bed, I checked my phone. There was an audio message from Rosie in response to one I'd sent her at dinner the previous evening before heading to the South Rim.

As I listened, I walked over to the window to try to see the sky beyond the brick wall and then started packing up my things. Rosie reminded me that I had indeed made progress since the funeral, and that in recovery we talk about progress, not perfection. Then she closed in typical Rosie fashion with "So take that progress, let go of perfection, and go get your kicks on Route 66."

I finished packing up my gear and got on the road just before seven. After I had been driving for about an hour, I started thinking about breakfast. I saw a sign for Winslow, Arizona, and thought of Nella, who had put the Eagles song on the playlist. I was humming

"Take It Easy" as I parked in front of a cool-looking diner with a Route 66 décor.

I ordered breakfast as the waitress turned over my cup and poured me a bottomless cup of coffee. I loved that aspect of diner culture, the coffee that never runs out. I sipped my coffee as I looked around at the paraphernalia on every inch of space on the wall and ceiling: old photos and road signs and old car and motorcycle parts hanging from the ceiling.

After watching the old TV show as a kid, I'd romanticized driving on Route 66. I hoped the drive would be as exciting as the fantasies I'd had.

I finished breakfast and got back on the road just after nine. After a couple of hours of driving, I could safely say that the fantasies far exceeded the drive itself. Most of the drive turned out to be boring; the terrain was monotonous and did nothing to improve my mood. As I looked out at the vast flatness, I couldn't help comparing it to what my future felt like: not a soul in sight, drab, and unexciting.

When I got to Santa Fe, I parked near the central plaza and gratefully got out of the car to stretch my legs and wander around. I saw a woman selling exquisite turquoise jewelry in the Plaza and went closer to take a look.

"Oh, I love those earrings," I said as I picked up a pair of chunky turquoise and silver earrings.

"Feel free to try them on. There is a mirror right over there so you can see how they look," the woman said, looking up to smile, then returning to the bracelet that she was working on.

I tried on the earrings; I loved the weight of them and how they hung just right. I tilted my head to the left and the right. I thought of the money I had just spent on a new tire and took the earrings off, disappointed. I handed them back to the woman and walked away. Then I thought, *Ah, the hell with it*, and walked back. I'd much rather share my money with this artist than with the creepy mechanic . . . and the earrings were a lot more fun than the tire. "On second thought, I'll take them," I said, and handed her the money.

I walked away clutching the earrings and smiling. It felt good to do something nice for myself.

By the time I got to my accommodation in Taos, the temperature was dropping. I slipped a sweatshirt on before locking my car.

The place that I had booked was a room in a large pueblo-style house with a view of the Sangre de Cristo Mountains. The late afternoon shadows had a purplish glow, and the light was magnificent. I could understand why so many artists ended up in Taos.

As I walked up to the gate, I noticed a car parked in the driveway with a bumper sticker that read: Practice Random Acts of Kindness. And when I reached the gate, there was a small sign announcing that the proprietor was a healer who did private sessions at the house.

*Hmm I wonder what that means,* I thought.

Before I could knock, a woman wearing a flowing, lavender and turquoise caftan opened the door and welcomed me.

"Come in, come in. Don't mind Rusty," she said by way of introducing her orange-and-white dog. "He's harmless and just wants to say hello." She pushed him with her foot before he could jump on me.

I walked into the tiled entryway and looked around. The late-afternoon light streamed in behind me and made the terra-cotta tiles look luminescent. The light hit the Southwest paintings on the wall like a spotlight. The yellow ochre, peach, and mauve seemed to glow.

"I'm Saskia," the woman said as she offered me her hand. Her colorful caftan, although flowing around her arms and legs, fought to contain her full breasts and hips, and the butterfly clip on top of her head was losing the battle to hold her wavy, copper colored hair as several tendrils snuck out in different directions.

"Meg," I answered as I shook her hand. I noticed the small sign asking me to remove my shoes. I slipped my feet out of my Birken-stocks and nudged them toward the wall, hoping that Rusty wasn't the type of dog who liked to chew on shoes.

"Follow me and I'll show you to your room."

The walls were white plaster, and the tiled floor was cool on my feet as I followed Saskia down the wide hallway. The room was open and light, with high, wood-beamed ceilings. I was so grateful I had come early as I mentally compared this room to the room I had left this morning.

"Oh, I am so glad I decided to come a day early. I feel so much better already. This room is wonderful."

"You're actually quite lucky. The room had been booked for one more day, but the people who were here decided to leave a day early, so it was available. I rarely have a vacancy in the summer. Taos is quite popular as I'm sure you know," Saskia said as she opened the French doors looking out toward the mountains. "But there are no mistakes in the Universe," she continued, "and I can tell that you need to be here. I could hear it in your voice when you called yesterday, and I could just feel it in your energy. I'm glad I could accommodate you. Having three nights here will help you unwind and heal." She paused and looked me up and down. "Why don't you take a shower now and wander out when you are ready. Then we can have a nice cup of tea out on the terrace. I brew a lovely sagebrush tea; it is a little bitter, but it has wonderful healing properties, and it is delicious with a dollop of desert-flower honey."

Then Saskia turned on her heel, closing the door behind her.

After that barrage of info, I felt like I had to shake my head to clear it. I walked over to the bed, thinking I might just lie down for a minute to rest after the long drive, but I fell asleep almost immediately.

By the time I opened my eyes again, the room was dark, and I could hear the faint cry of coyotes in the distance. It took me a few minutes to remember where I was. I looked at my phone; it was after nine o'clock. *Too late for that healing tea, no doubt*, I thought. So I decided to take a bath. I located some bath salts in the cabinet under the sink and felt giddy at the thought of soaking in the bath, what luxury. By the time I finished, I felt relaxed enough to go back to bed and read for a while before turning off the light and going back to sleep.

I woke up and looked out the window to a startlingly blue sky the next morning. I could smell coffee and hear someone in the kitchen.

I wasn't even in the kitchen yet when Saskia started talking to me.

"So happy you've had such a good rest," she called out. "I could tell that you were going to fall asleep early; the energy radiating off of you last night was palpable. So I just sipped my sagebrush tea alone on the terrace and listened to the coyotes. Did you hear them last night? They were singing up a storm. I think they must be mating out there and crying out to each other. Not to mention the moon last night. Did you see it? It was like a spotlight in the sky. I hope it didn't keep you awake. But no, of course it didn't. You were asleep so early. You look so much more rested this morning than you did last night. I could just see in your aura that you were exhausted and needed to rest. I forgot to tell you yesterday that there is a bathtub in your bathroom, but I'm sure you found it."

She looked at me and smiled. "I'll put some herbs in the bathroom today while you're out so you can add them to your bath tonight."

I looked around the kitchen; much of the wall and counter space was filled with angels and dream catchers threatening to catch them midflight. "Now, are you a coffee drinker? The coffee is freshly brewed. Or I can brew up some of my sagebrush tea if you prefer. I myself am an herbal tea drinker; I never touch coffee, it bruises my spirit, and I think it hampers my ability to heal. But of course, I always keep it on hand to offer to my guests."

"I'm a coffee drinker," I said, looking directly at Saskia, almost daring her to challenge it. Saskia poured my coffee from a carafe and handed it to me. "There's milk and honey on the table. I refuse to keep sugar in my house; it's poison to our bodies. Now have a seat and I'll bring you some breakfast. Would you like to eat in the kitchen? Or would you prefer to eat on the terrace? It's an absolutely beautiful morning; let's have breakfast on the terrace. The mornings are so lovely this time of year. Of course by midday, the sun is fierce. So whatever you're thinking of doing today, you should plan on getting out soon. I'll just whip up some eggs and toast and bring it all out in a jiffy. Go ahead and grab the jam and butter from the table there and bring it out if you don't mind. I'll be out in a minute with plates and cutlery and glasses for juice. I squeeze my own citrus juice, that way we aren't consuming any extra sugar. We all have to do what we can to keep our systems clean. And don't worry about the eggs; they're free-range, from a woman up the road who keeps chickens. I would never buy battery-hen eggs. More poison for our system. And for toast I have a few choices, all locally freshly baked. There is a multigrain loaf or sourdough, or I can offer you gluten-free if you like. Are you gluten-free?"

I said that multigrain would be fine, and I took my coffee, with the butter and jam, and headed out to the terrace before Saskia could continue. I took a few deep breaths and looked out over the high desert from the terrace. It really was a stunning view with the wide-open blue sky and the silvery sagebrush.

"I bought this place for this terrace and view, to be honest," Saskia said as she walked out onto the terrace, Rusty following closely behind. "I decided that I could redo the interior, which I did, believe me, as long as I had this view to sustain me." She put the plates down on the table and took the cutlery wrapped in cloth napkins out of the big pocket in her flowy skirt and set them next to the plates. "Sit, sit." I wasn't sure if she was talking to me or the dog, as Rusty immediately sat down next to her, obviously waiting to be fed. "Let's eat while it's still hot."

I ate while Saskia kept up a constant commentary about Taos and the surrounding area, alternating bites of toast for herself and then Rusty. She seemed to have a strong opinion about half the population there as she told me where to go and where to avoid.

I had serious second thoughts about staying two more nights with this woman, whose voice was beginning to feel like sandpaper on my brain. My room was lovely, but I wondered if I could put up with the nonstop chatter from her. I decided I'd just have to tolerate it over breakfast, get out quickly for the day, and then sequester myself in my room at night.

I was just about to interrupt her to say I wanted to get on the road when Saskia abruptly stopped talking and started stacking the plates and cups to take into the kitchen. "Well, you best be on your way, otherwise the heat will be intolerable."

I blinked, feeling like she had read my mind.

"Will you be home for dinner tonight?"

"Oh, no," I said hastily. "I'm planning to be out all day. I'll stop off somewhere for a light dinner before I come home. Don't wait up for me; I'm sure I'll be bushed by the end of the day."

I helped Saskia clear the table, hurried to my room to gather what I might need for the day, and got out as quickly as I could.

I decided to head out to the Taos Pueblo; fifteen minutes later I arrived, paid the fee to enter, and read a bit about the history. The multistoried adobe buildings had been continuously inhabited for over a thousand years; how was that even possible? There were still many families with over 150 Puebloans who lived within the pueblo. I wondered what it would be like to live communally, to work and live together with a group of people, day in and day out. I wasn't sure I had it in me, but I kind of liked the idea of a close-knit community.

I felt awkward being a tourist in someone's home and community, but I also knew that the people who lived here depended on tourist dollars, so I was conflicted. I went into a curio shop, hoping to find something to buy to support the community. There was beautiful pottery, but that didn't make sense to travel with, so I bought some silver earrings for Nella and Rosie.

As I was coming out of the shop, a woman walked by with a young child strapped to her back with a colorful piece of cloth. The child dropped a small doll made from burlap and was reaching back for it. I picked it up and hurried to catch up to the mother and child.

"Excuse me," I said, slightly out of breath after jogging to catch up, "your baby dropped this." I held out the doll to the mother.

The mother thanked me, took the doll, and passed it over her shoulder to the child who reached for the doll and stared at me. I smiled and waved at the child as the woman walked away. The child turned her head and continued to watch me.

A lump formed in my throat; I missed my own babies so much. It had been many years since I had carried my sons on my back, but I could still feel that hefty weight, their damp, warm heads as they slept against my body.

I found a bench in the shade and took out my phone to send an audio message to my boys. I told them I missed them, but found it hard to put into words the ache I was feeling after watching the mother with her baby. I told them about Taos and the pueblo and finally took a selfie with the pueblo in the background and sent it off. Then I sent the same pic with a short note to Nella: "Made it to Taos, will call soon for a catch up, promise."

My moods were like a stormy sea, would they always be like this? One day feeling powerless and sobbing, the next day full of angst, longing for days past. Would I be alone for the rest of my life, always looking forward to the days that my sons would visit me? I had a horrible vision of myself sitting in a rocking chair on a porch, looking out, waiting for a visitor. I shook my head to clear it. Christ, when did I get so morose?

As I continued to sit on the bench, watching the Puebloans work,

I pondered that question, trying to remember when I actually did start feeling depressed. I had been at my job for over a decade, and it certainly didn't give me much joy as I sat in the little cubicle in the soulless high-rise, figuring out insurance claims with only a little cactus and a picture of my sons from about seven years ago to keep me company. I was happy for a while when I met my fun-loving ex-husband, and thought I had won the lottery when I had my children. But the marriage soon lost its shine the more my ex drank and the later he stayed out while the kids and I sat home. It had been a blast when we were young party animals together, but it was very different once we were a bit older and had a family. After we divorced, life as a single parent was much harder than I thought it would be. Days turned into weeks, then into years, and there was never enough time or money; the laundry pile never seemed to get smaller, and time for me to just relax never materialized. And yet, once the boys got older and left home, I was so painfully lonely, and I longed for the noise and the mess. And I wondered if I'd ever find a partner to share the journey with, but how do older people even meet? Tinder and Bumble were not made for our wrinkled, clumsy fingers to swipe; the whole idea of online dating felt pathetic and cringeworthy.

I thought I had made peace with being alone, but as I sat there, I wasn't so sure.

As I walked back to my car, I realized that I had the answer to my question about when I had started feeling morose and depressed: it had always been there. It was the thing that I had sought to drown out with alcohol. Sometimes it got buried or even disappeared for months at a time, and I was able to pretend everything was OK, but it always resurfaced.

I felt the familiar knot in my stomach and realized that I needed to break this cycle. I had sought to numb that pain for years with so many self-defeating patterns, but this trip was highlighting my need to heal old wounds that kept me stuck. It was time for change.

———

When I got back to Taos, I had dinner at a small café, taking my time to eat, with the very clear intention of avoiding Saskia. I came back to the house well after dark and slipped in quietly. I was afraid that Rusty might start barking, but the house stayed quiet. I softly crept to my room, feeling like a teenager sneaking in past curfew.

I sat with the light off and looked out the window at the moon for a while before crawling into bed.


Before venturing into the kitchen for breakfast the next morning, I did some research online about hikes in the area. I read about a nearby waterfall that sounded beautiful and hoped I might even be able to go for a swim. When I walked into the kitchen, Saskia was at the stove, talking back to a person on the radio. I wondered if she ever stopped talking. I contemplated turning around and sneaking out to have breakfast in town, but breakfast was already being made, and after all, the meal was included in the price.

"Good morning, Meg," she said above the radio. "Let me turn this down. The announcer on this station is a real jerk, and I enjoy arguing with him in the morning." She chuckled. "You must have thought I was a bit loony, carrying on like that. But anyway, how was your day yesterday? You mentioned that you might head up to the pueblo; did you get up there? I should have told you about a few places to stop near there. I have several friends who live in the area who are artists, and you could have stopped by their galleries. One friend of mine paints amazing landscapes of the area. I have a few of her paintings up in the house; I love that one in the entryway that you would have seen as you came in. She's very talented. She's self-taught, you see, and Spirit just moves through her as she paints. I also have a friend who is a masseuse if you need any bodywork done. She's amazing too. I hold so much tension in my back and shoulders, and she just releases it. It's wonderful. When I do my healing sessions, a lot of tension leaves the body of the person that I am working on, and it can lodge in me, so I need to release it quickly or it can become debilitating. Oh dear, the eggs are burning . . ." Saskia grabbed a towel and took the pan off the burner. "No worries. I'll take this omelet. What would you like in yours? I've got peppers and tomatoes and cheese and salsa. I put it all in mine, shall I do the same for yours?"

I nodded and hoped I could just get my coffee and escape to the terrace.

"Now, you just help yourself to some coffee there, and I'll be out with breakfast in a jiffy," she said, once again as though she were reading my thoughts.

*How does she get into my head?* I wondered. Was it really happening or was I just imagining it? Was she some kind of genuine woo-woo witch? Or was this all a Taos-themed gimmick?

"Shall I take the butter and jam out again?" I asked as I poured my coffee, trying not sound as exasperated as I felt.

"Yes, please. And take the knives and forks with you as well if you can manage it. I'll be out in a few minutes." Saskia bent down and fed Rusty some of the omelet she had just made and was already turning up the radio and talking back to the announcer before I was even out of the room.

I was at the table pouring the juice when Saskia came out and put a plate in front of me. It was a large plate, full to overflowing with two pieces of toast and a huge omelet. "Now you just eat what you can," Saskia said before she sat down. "Anything you don't eat, I'll just pass on to my neighbor. She keeps chickens; that's where I buy my free-range eggs. She feeds her hens all kinds of scraps, including eggs and even the eggshells. I asked her once, 'But isn't that like cannibalism?' but she assured me that it doesn't bother the chickens at all, that it's even good for them. Have you ever heard that? Chickens eating eggs?

To me that just seems wrong, like eating their own young. You know what I mean? But she's been keeping chickens for decades, so who am I to argue? And her eggs are so good, the yolks are such a dark rich color; you can tell by the color of the omelet, not a pale anemic yellow at all, but almost orange, so healthy. Go ahead and taste it; you can taste the health of the eggs in the omelet. So anyway, where are you headed today?" She paused, took a big bite of her omelet, and stared at me.

I waited to see if she was just going to carry on talking or if this really was a question. When the silence lasted for more than just a few seconds, I answered. "I decided to go for a hike up to El Salto Falls. It looks like a lovely area, and I'd love to swim at some falls; that just sounds wonderful to me."

"Oh, that is a beautiful area up there, about a half hour's drive, very picturesque. And you'll be passing right through El Prado; now El Prado itself is not picturesque at all. It's just a spot on the map, a sneeze-and-you'll-miss-it kind of place. However, that's where my friend has her gallery; you should absolutely stop along the way. I'll call her and tell her you'll be in." Saskia paused and fed some of her omelet to Rusty, who had been hanging out under the table, whining at her feet. "But before you go, I think I should do a healing on you. Your spirit seems to be sagging a bit."

Against my better judgement, I asked: "What does that mean, that my spirit is sagging?"

"Well, your aura is a bit cloudy, and your colors are not very vibrant, even now. I mean, when you arrived at my door, your aura was grey and murky brown, indicating blocked energy and distrust; that you're afraid of losing your power, a very weak energy. I could hear it on the phone when you called, and then I confirmed it in spades when you arrived and I saw you. And yeah, you were tired as well, which certainly impacts your aura. And today, although it is much better than it was, it's still not a healthy hue; it's dim, indicating a weak energy as I said. I can do an energy clearing, which will certainly be a boost, but I would also say kindness would be a big help. I'm not saying that you aren't kind to people, that's not my point at all, but going out of your way to be extra kind would be very helpful to your energy. Practicing random acts of kindness is always helpful. I even have a bumper sticker on my car and I tell anyone who will listen that going out of your way to be kind is always a healing thing to do. But I get the feeling, mainly, that you are not very kind to yourself. Is that true? Are you kind to yourself, Meg?"

"Uh . . ." I felt a blush rising up my body and looked down at my plate, hoping that Saskia would keep talking about something else. I tried to eat more eggs, but my throat was too tight for food. I buttoned my shirt up to my throat like I could somehow shield myself from her invasive eyes, and it also served to hide the blush creeping up from my chest. Did she know all the unkind thoughts I had had about her. Was I really that transparent? Could she really read my mind? I just wanted to get out of the house.

"Oh dear, now I've made you feel uncomfortable. My friend, the masseuse I told you about, keeps telling me that I've got to stop reading people without their permission. She says that I'm intrusive and that it's not fair to use my gift on others without giving them some say in the matter. And now I can see that you've shut down and are withdrawing and I apologize. But please let me do a simple, quick cleanse for you, on the house. It would be great to do before you go out for your hike. That would be the perfect thing before your swim at the waterfall. A swim at the falls is such a cleansing thing to do. So if I do a clearing first, your soul will surely thank you." She took another huge bite of her omelet.

I didn't particularly want an energy cleanse, whatever that was, but I also felt guilty, like Saskia had been reading all of my judgmental thoughts, and I somehow owed it to her to let her do a healing on me. So I reluctantly agreed to it and asked what it entailed.

"Oh, don't worry, you don't have to do a single thing. You just lay down on my massage table, and I'll do all the work. What I'd like you to do, if you don't mind, is to take a quick shower and visualize yourself washing away all the stress and negativity in your body. Picture washing that dull grayish aura right down the drain, and surround yourself with glowing white light. Then put on a robe or loose clothing and come into my healing studio. I'll be in there smudging the room, lighting some candles, and getting it ready. My studio is out behind the house. Go out the back door from the kitchen and down the path; you can't miss it."

My shoulders instinctively drew in protectively; this was way outside my comfort zone. I also wanted to get on the road so I wasn't hiking in the heat of the day.

"Don't worry, this won't take long. And you'll have that wonderful swim in the pool by the falls to cool off."

"How do you do that?" I exclaimed.

"Do what?" Saskia asked.

"Oh, never mind." I shook my head and headed to my room.


I was only going to jump in and out of the shower, but then I thought, *What the hell, what can it hurt?* So I closed my eyes and tried to picture a dull grey film rinsing off my skin and circling down the drain. The vision was a bit cloudy, but I did my best. Then I dried off, changed into loose clothes, and walked out the back door, following the scent of burning sage.

As I walked into Saskia's studio, my eyes took a minute to adjust to the dim lighting; I saw candles and crystals through the hazy smoke. There was a massage table in the middle of the room draped with a lavender cloth; Saskia had her eyes closed and was waving a tightly tied bunch of burning white sage over the table.

She kept her eyes closed as she motioned to me to join her at the table. "Please get on to the table, face down."

I crawled onto the table and put my face in the small hole in the table looking down at a big, jagged, purple crystal.

"I'll start by smudging you with sage to help cleanse your aura and clear the negative energy. I'm using an eagle feather to help circulate the smoke to aid in the process. I've put an amethyst below you; you can focus on it while you are on your stomach."

Saskia went silent after that. I closed my eyes and slowly began to feel a strange buzzing sensation in my body, like I was getting a small electrical charge. I felt a bit dozy, but just when I was about to fall asleep, Saskia asked me to roll over.

I rolled onto my back, and Saskia gently lifted my head and placed a small pillow under it. Then she placed three crystals on my belly; quite suddenly it felt like a small swarm of bees were let loose in my stomach. It wasn't totally unpleasant, but it was very strange.

I watched as Saskia started at my feet and used the feather to push the smoke around my body. The buzzing sensation followed the smoke, and soon my whole body was gently vibrating. I felt incredibly relaxed and light, as if I were floating. By the time she reached my head, I felt like she was inside a cloud: everything was hazy and soft.

"Now you just take your time getting up. And I've left you a glass of water by the door; please drink it all. I'll be in the kitchen." Saskia quietly left the room and closed the door behind her.

I continued to lie on the table for several minutes. When I finally sat up, I was lightheaded and slightly dizzy but felt really rested and clear. I got up and drank the water; I hadn't realized how thirsty I was. I walked back up the path and into the kitchen.

"Well, that's much better," Saskia said when she saw me. "The grey is gone, and you've got a vibrant yellow and orange glow around you now—vitality and optimism. Ah yes, much better indeed. Now go spend some time in nature; that will be perfect, and take a long swim in the waters by the falls, a wonderful follow-up to the healing. And please be kind to yourself today, be gentle and say nice things to yourself. And if you have a chance, practice random acts of kindness to the others you meet on your path. Now I've got to take a shower and lie down. Come on, Rusty, let's go take a nap." She walked out of the kitchen with Rusty trotting behind her.

———

On the way out of town, I stopped at a small café to get some coffee to perk me up for the drive. Behind me in line, there was a young, harried-looking mother with two small children clinging to her. After I paid for my coffee, I gave the barista twenty dollars and told her to please pay the bill for the woman and children and to keep the change for herself. I walked out without looking back.

As I drove out of town, I felt a smile spread across my face.

I sipped my coffee and thought about the whole experience. What the hell had just happened? I had to admit my body felt different, more electrified somehow, although my skeptic brain tried to explain that away with the coffee. Was I now somehow a woman who believed in auras and angels? Would I start buying crystals and going to full moon rituals? But I did feel different, I could not ignore it; not only was my body buzzing a bit, but I also felt clearer somehow, like I'd put on a pair of glasses with the perfect prescription.

El Salto Falls is actually composed of several separate falls. If I had been more adventurous and a lot fitter, I would have tried to explore the whole area, but I decided I'd find one waterfall with a decent size pool and just hang out there. The first falls I hit actually had two waterfalls coming down into a small pool. It was quiet and peaceful, but I decided to explore a bit further.

The huge boulders that were scattered throughout the canyon made the hike interesting and a bit challenging, but I was glad that I persevered. When I arrived at the second waterfall, I knew I had found my swimming spot. Three waterfalls streamed down the flat ochre rock cliff into a blue-green pool. The triple waterfall was tucked away and surrounded by trees.

I found a flat boulder, stripped down to my bathing suit, and stepped into the water. The water was clean and clear and cool. I plunged in and felt its silkiness flow over me. I floated with my head back and looked up at the falls, watching a hawk circling overhead, time seeming to stand still. When I finally got out of the water, I lay back on the sun-warmed boulder. I felt light and airy. I had never thought twice about my aura or carrying any negative energy, but whatever Saskia had done had made a huge difference. What I felt was cleansed.


On the way home, I stopped and bought a couple of things for the trip to Boulder the next day and picked up a few unplanned items too.

When I got back to Saskia's, the house was dark and silent. I quietly went to the kitchen, found a vase in a cabinet, and filled it with the flowers I had bought. I found a small pad and pen on the counter. "Thank you for your kindness, Saskia," I wrote. "I shall pay it forward."

*Day Seven, Eight, and Nine—Taos New Mexico*

*What an amazing several days I have had in Taos. I've learned a lot being here. One of the things I've learned is that I'm not very tolerant; in fact, I'm quite judgmental. Not just about others, but about myself as well. Last time I heard from Rosie, she reminded me to practice progress, not perfection. With that lens, I am looking at my judgement about other people as well, most specifically the woman I stayed with here, Saskia. I had so much judgement about her—about how much she talked and how invasive I thought she was—and yet, she turned out to be so important on my journey. First of all, she has a glorious house, which felt healing in and of itself. And her gift of a "cleansing" was amazing! My body just feels different after that experience, lighter and more fluid. It was wild! But most important was the secret she taught me— about kindness, toward others and toward myself. She was a great model. So thank you, Saskia, for your kindness and for sharing your secret with me.*

*Secret #4*

*Kindness—random acts of kindness and just plain old kindness to others and to myself.*

# Trauma, Addiction, and Connection

BOULDER, CO

## CHAPTER 7

> "The opposite of addiction isn't sobriety. It's connection."
> —JOHANN HARI

As I drove across the Rio Grande Gorge Bridge, it was obvious that it was a real feat of engineering; the height alone made me dizzy. I was grateful that Saskia had suggested this route to Boulder and that I'd left extra early to watch the sunrise over the gorge—another suggestion from her. It was like a Technicolor big-budget movie scene, hard to believe it was real and not drug induced; orange, magenta, and deep blue in the sky, creating an otherworldly purplish glow in the gorge.

Once I had reached the other side of the bridge, I pulled over and sat on the hood of the mustang, eating the breakfast Saskia had handed me on my way out. I sipped the coffee she made me as I watched the colors lose their intensity as the sun rose higher in the sky. I took a deep breath and let the beauty settle around me. This was why I was doing this road trip, this was what I had been hoping for: basking in beauty, letting the sunrise paint my skin, and feeling the warmth of the kindness from Saskia spread through my body. I let myself sink into the deep gratitude I felt.

When the sun was well risen, I got back in the car and headed north. Next stop, Buena Vista, about three hours away.

The terrain changed as I drove through the Pike and San Isabel National Forest. The landscape became lusher with more trees and water, more greens and blues.

I felt my spirit being nourished with the changing landscape, like a plant that had been forgotten suddenly springing back to life with a good watering. When I reached Buena Vista, I realized how thirsty I was, and I stopped at a little market to get some juice. While there, I asked about some easy hikes nearby. The woman at the shop recommended The Barbara Whipple Trail; she said it was an easy but scenic walk.

Perfect.

The five-kilometer hike was what I was hoping for, relatively easy and cool next to the river, offering a clear view of the mountain range in the distance. At one point I took a selfie with the mountains in the background and sent the picture and a long audio to my sons.

After I sent the audio, I looked up the number that Rosie had sent and called Rachel in Boulder. I let her know I would be getting to Boulder that afternoon and asked about a good women's meeting. She told me there was a great one the following day and invited me to her house for dinner.

I drove straight through to Boulder after finishing the hike and made it to my hotel in less than three hours. Although the hotel was a faceless chain, the shower was hot and strong, and I let the water ease the tension in my shoulders and back.

As the water beat against my torso, I reflected on the last shower

I'd taken, at Saskia's. *Was that really only yesterday?* I felt like I was in a different body, certainly a different headspace. Not only the lightness of being that I had felt at the falls, but my head also felt clearer, less scattered and certainly less negative. As I stood under the shower, the realization hit me: not only had Saskia's shower washed a possible muddy aura residue away, but my time in Taos had cracked me open. That's what it felt like, that this water was hitting a fresher, softer me, like a hard casing that I thought had been protecting me was gone.

By the time I was out of the shower and changed, it was time to go to Rachel's.

Rachel opened the door wide and welcomed me with a warm hug. It looked like she was still in her work clothes, tall and professional looking, with heels under her maroon pleated pants. Her hair was short, peppered with grey. But it was her eyes that drew my attention; they seemed to sparkle with flecks of gold. The word that came to mind when I looked at her was "regal."

"I'm so glad you made it. Can I get you a cold soda with lime?"

I followed Rachel through her house to the kitchen, where she poured us both a drink.

"You have a lovely home, Rachel. How long have you lived in Boulder?"

"Oh, I've been here for about six years now. I was teaching at a small university in the Midwest and wanted to work somewhere with a bit more going on, and I was lucky there was an opening in my field here at the university."

"Rosie mentioned that you're a professor—specializing in addiction, right?" I asked. "What led you there?"

"My own addiction of course." Rachel laughed as she picked up the drinks; I followed her through the sliding doors to her deck. As we sat down, she continued, "I was teaching Sociology when I got sober the first time. The stress and demands were so intense that I convinced myself that a glass of wine and the occasional Valium were not a problem but were instead a necessity and well deserved. And it wasn't long before I was in the middle of full-blown addiction again. I hid it for quite a while; I thought I was doing well keeping it from my students and colleagues, but it wasn't long before the head of my department called me on it. Apparently, some of my students had complained. So I put myself in treatment, went back to 12-Step meetings and started studying addiction."

I took a corn chip from the bowl, dipped it into the salsa that was on the table, and listened as she continued.

"I found Dr. Gabor Maté's work really resonated with me. He calls for a more compassionate approach toward addiction and believes that the source of addiction is almost always trauma, which usually occurs in the early childhood environment; he emphasized that we need to understand 'not why the addiction but why the pain.'"

I nodded; that fit with what Rosie and I often talked about. She and I had similar backgrounds—growing up in alcoholic families, constantly on edge, waiting for disaster, not knowing if plans made would be carried through or cancelled, wondering if a meal would be eaten in silence or end up a shouting match with things broken. From a very young age, we had both learned to be hypervigilant, expecting the worst. We learned to people-please, thinking if we were just good enough and took care of everything well enough that there would be peace. But peace was always elusive. Rosie and I acknowledged that the trauma of our childhoods still stuck to us like a cloak.

Rachel continued: "I once heard a podcast with Dr. Maté and Dr. Peter Levine discussing trauma and the disconnection to self that happens after a traumatic event. They explained that we disconnect from ourselves because it would be too painful if we didn't. They said something that I really connected with, that trauma is not what happens to you, but what happens inside you as a result of what happens to you. So in essence the trauma is not the external event itself, but the internal response to it. And in addiction, we not only disconnect from the pain, but also seek maladaptive ways to ease or numb it. To understand addiction, we need to ask what relief the addict finds, or hopes to find, in the drug or the addictive behavior. The problem though, as you and I well understand, is that the attempt to escape from pain is what creates more pain."

That made sense; I nodded as I leaned forward.

"But," Rachel paused and looked at me, "this trauma approach did not align with the classic 12-Step model, and that really floored me. I mean, 12-Step meetings were keeping me clean and sober, and it frightened me to hear anything that challenged the accepted philosophy."

I felt my breathing getting shallower, and leaned slightly away from her like I could avoid where she was leading. "I know where you're going with this, and I'm struggling. I know the AA party line is that alcoholism is a disease that we are born with, and there is often no room for discussion of childhood trauma or anything else. I loathed being in some of the meetings where old men said all I had to do was put a plug in the jug and not drink and everything would be fine when it clearly wasn't. And of course, the patriarchy that the program is steeped in is crazy-making. However, it's still helping me stay sober."

Rachel nodded. "Dr. Maté and Dr. Peter Levine both agreed that 12-Step is an amazing process, very helpful in so many ways . . ."

"I hear a 'but' coming . . ."

Rachel smiled and continued, "But . . . it's limited if that's all you have. If we are only around people who identify themselves with their maladaptation to their trauma, then it's not enough. We need more to heal the trauma itself. And this information is hard to hear for people in 12-Step rooms if they believe that meetings are all they need to recover."

I stood up and walked over to the fence at the edge of the deck. I didn't feel like I could sit still, there was a knot in my stomach, and my back started to cramp up. I twisted my back around a bit, but I motioned to Rachel to continue.

"Are you alright, Meg?"

I walked back to the table and took a big sip of sparkling water. "Yeah, I'm OK, but this information is difficult to hear, like you're telling me that what has kept me sober is wrong somehow. I mean I know I've been searching for answers, and what you are saying is not totally new to me, but it brings up a lot of fear when you say the 12 steps aren't enough."

Rachel's eyes were kind. "I understand that; I felt the same way. But I came to believe that it's also freeing; we don't have to replace 12-Step meetings, but we have permission to do more, to acknowledge that the 12 steps alone aren't enough. To me this understanding shined a light on what I had been experiencing, that I need more than just talking about my addiction."

I took another deep breath and looked out at the trees beyond her property. I rolled my neck and heard the creaking as I released the stress. "Yeah, I do understand that, and in a way, it's comforting to hear you describe this because it's been a struggle for me too, but I still find it confronting. As I said, the patriarchy and so much of the closed-minded behavior was hard to be around. However, when I quit going to meetings, it wasn't long before I started drinking again. It feels like a real catch-22. So this information is disquieting." I sat down, dipped another chip in salsa and ate it.

"Yes, I understand. It is uncomfortable," Rachel said gently. "At the same time, it's not surprising that you found your way back to the rooms looking for help and community; I think it's pretty well accepted now that to recover from addiction, you need connection."

I nodded; connection was definitely an important piece for me. Rachel went on to describe more of her research, finding that we absolutely need connection, but many women found that 12-Step recovery was not a good fit for them—whether it was because of the patriarchal tone, the "religious element," or the fact that they just didn't feel comfortable in the meetings. "One of the books that helped me get past that strict patriarchy was *A Woman's Way*

*Through the Twelve Steps* by Stephanie Covington. And several of the younger women I interviewed liked Holly Whitaker's *Quit Like a Woman*, with the wonderful subtitle: *The Radical Choice to Not Drink in a Culture Obsessed with Alcohol."*

My stomach growled and Rachel shook her head. "Oh, I'm so sorry! I've been blathering on and have failed to give you the dinner I promised," she said as she pushed her chair out and got up. "Let's bring the food out here to eat. It's such a lovely evening."

We brought the food out to the table and served ourselves. I took a bite of the warm sourdough bread and groaned with pleasure. "Oh my God, this is delicious!"

"Thanks, I made it with a sourdough starter I've had for a few years. Glad you like it."

I buttered another thick slice of bread. "Please tell me more about your research," I said after I swallowed.

"Well, as I mentioned earlier, it's the work of Gabor Maté that really spoke to me. I think he shows pretty conclusively that in reality there is only one addiction process, and that is the self-soothing of deep-seated fears and discomforts. His research found that addiction is about the emotional pain behind the behavior. He says that confronting the past and really looking at the circumstances that drove us addicts to self-medicate to the point of death is necessary to fully recover."

"Yeah, that feels so true," I said, nodding my head.

"So in essence," Rachel continued, "whatever it is I'm addicted to, and for me that list is long, it's not what it is but what it does. Basically, anything we've ever craved or been addicted to helped us numb out or escape emotional pain. It gave us peace of mind and a sense of control. And my addictive behavior, though damaging in the long term, soothed me in the short term. Maté explains that the primary drive is to regulate a bad situation to something more bearable. He argues that our brains are wired for joy and we seek to be soothed. And if our peace or joy are threatened by trauma in our past that we've not resolved, we resort to addictions to restore what we truly crave."

This all rang so painfully true. I had spent my life dealing with various addictions to deal with my past trauma. I stood up and looked up at the sky full of stars, aware of the familiar tightening in my body when I was facing an uncomfortable truth. I sat back down and took another bite of bread. "Everything you're saying makes so much sense. What I've been noticing on this trip is that things that I used to think soothed me now have more of an adverse effect, now that I'm a bit more conscious, so I need to pay a bit more attention and not just do old habits because I'm uncomfortable," I said and looked at the bread I was eating rather addictively and took another bite.

"Exactly. And that reveals a great deal about addiction in general, which as I said, Maté defines as any behavior that gives us temporary relief and pleasure, even though it almost always has negative consequences. And even with those negative consequences, we will come back to it again and again until, as you say, we become more conscious. Maté has said, 'It takes a lot of work to wake up as a human being; it's a lot easier to stay asleep than to wake up.' It seems obvious to me that addicts shouldn't be shamed or criminalized, but instead be treated in the same way we treat anyone suffering from cancer or any other disease: not with blame, but rather with compassion, sympathy and medical intervention.

I closed my eyes and nodded. This was something else that Rosie and I talked about a lot. People with addiction needed to be treated with respect and compassion, not harsh punishment. The so-called war on drugs that seeks to prevent the use of certain drugs, primarily through punishment and coercion, has been an obvious failure. People suffering from addiction need care and connection. Rosie and I had watched a great TED Talk by Johann Hari called "Everything You Think You Know about Addiction Is Wrong" that described this beautifully.

I took a sip of water and asked what brought her back to 12-Step rooms.

"Well, while some of the archaic language and the patriarchy almost drove me away, I missed the camaraderie, and I personally really like the spiritual element of the rooms. But I definitely know that I need a combination of things for healthy recovery. I have to take what I need and leave the rest; that goes for the literature I read, as well as the 12-Step meetings that I attend. What I've found, for me as well as from the research, is that the key is finding community; you need to find the people that create that support."

"Me too." I nodded vigorously. "I'm attracted to the spiritual element of 12-Step recovery, but I find that I need to sew together several approaches, kind of like a quilt—a patchwork approach, if you will."

Rachel smiled. "I love that, 'a patchwork approach'—can I quote you?"

"Absolutely!" I said, and we clinked our glasses together. "Your information affirms what I have felt for a while. I need more than simply going to meetings. It was those damned old men telling me that *all* I needed to do was to go to meetings and not pick up that led me to pick up. I realize that I need more than just the 12 steps. I need to access a whole basket of tools. Just on this trip alone, I'm realizing what it is that makes me feel good and what it is that I do that makes me feel like crap. For example, I've been really noticing recently that what I eat impacts my moods. I mean, I know that's pretty basic, but I guess I just never paid much attention to that."

"Oh, yes. There is so much research on food and addiction."

I grimaced a bit as I chewed another huge bite of bread and tried to hide the bulge in my mouth.

Rachel continued, "Sugar cravings are especially rough when people stop drinking. There is an assumption that this craving is because your body is used to the high sugar content found in alcoholic drinks, and while that makes sense, research shows that there is a deeper link. I've read several studies that show that eating sweets causes your brain to release dopamine, which is the reward-based chemical that makes you feel good. In fact, sugar affects many of the same neural pathways in the brain as alcohol does." Rachel, smiling self-consciously, shook her head. "Sorry, when we start talking about all this, I get into my professorial mode. Of course, it's true, we just operate better on a healthier diet. But just because we know it, doesn't mean we do it."

"Boy that is for sure. When I was in Arches National Park recently, I felt despondent and lonely, so I ate a tub of ice cream." I rolled my eyes and took a sip of water. "Not surprisingly, I felt worse when the carton was empty, and there was a residual effect that lasted into the next day. Not just the overconsumption of sugar, although of course that's part of it, but overconsumption in general. And other things I'm noticing too, that either add to a positive mood or detract from it; hiking and being out in nature doesn't just make my body feel better, but my mood improves too, and I notice that I feel worse when I watch dumb videos than when I read or watch something inspirational. God, I sound so stupid as I'm listening to myself. This is all so obvious."

"No, you don't sound stupid at all," Rachel said gently. "Do you know how many people go to their graves without learning these important lessons? What other tools have you sewn into this patchwork approach."

I pushed the bread a bit further away to avoid temptation, then looked up at Rachel. "Well, I needed a shitload of counseling for my healing after I got into recovery. It was like I needed about a year to come out of the fog, then I needed to do some intense work to untangle some wires in my brain. And I need to meditate more, for sure, and connect to my higher self to take care of myself spiritually. And finally, something I've really noticed on this trip echoes what you were just saying, I need connection; I need to connect with like-minded people. When I go too long without connecting to people, I notice a very obvious drop in mood."

"Well said, Meg. Seems to me you have made some amazing discoveries on this recovery road trip of yours. Here's to you and the patches you've been collecting for that quilt," Rachel said, raising her glass.

"Oh, I wish I had learned all of this so many years ago," I said with a big exhale. "I feel like you just scraped off a huge layer of shame that I have been carrying around most of my life. And you know what else I'm just realizing now? After all this talk about the patriarchy and the number of old men who told me not to talk about emotions but to just do as I was told . . . I realize how much that was like my father." A shiver went up my spine. "Shit, I can't believe I never made that connection before. I feel like I might throw up."

Rachel came around the table, sat next to me, and put her arm around me. She didn't say a word, just sat there by my side, rubbing my shoulder.

We stayed outside until the chill of the evening and the mosquitoes drove us indoors.


When I opened my room's blackout curtains the next morning and looked out upon the day, it was drizzly and cloudy, which was surprising since Boulder is known for its sunshine—over three hundred days a year. But the drizzly weather was a good excuse to spend some time in a nearby museum. I decided to walk along the Boulder Creek Path to get to the Museum of Contemporary Art first. I had heard that the town was known for being very bikeable and walkable; it was great to see it all so accessible.

I changed my clothes, grabbed my raincoat, and headed out. It was damp and cool, a wonderful change from the hot desert environments I'd been in for the last several days.

First stop—coffee. I stopped at the library that was right on the path by the creek. I got a large coffee and a fresh muffin for breakfast at the library, then wandered the short distance to the art museum.

I loved the eclectic mix of contemporary art; there were a couple of regional exhibits and artists that were particularly innovative and interesting. One large installation with paintings in various shades of turquoise and orange and grey resembled what I imagine the origin of the universe might have looked like. The vibrant colors and interesting textures energized me; taking it all in was like drinking a large latté.

As I wandered around the different rooms in the museum, I realized that I had been ignoring my thirst for art and creativity. How had I lapsed to this point . . . to the point that I had lost that connection to creativity? I used to tell people that I used creativity to connect to my deepest sense of self. And yet, I had so easily abandoned it. At first, I had reasoned that, as a mother of young children, there was no time for any creative endeavors, that my sons took all of my time and energy. But now, with both of them grown and gone, I no longer had that excuse. Then it was work that left me exhausted at the end of the day. But I spent hours mindlessly scrolling through social media pages; I somehow found time for that. As I marveled at a metal sculpture with thrusting edges and interesting angles, I promised myself that I would spend more time being creative.

When my stomach started to rumble, I left the museum and found a café on Boulder's historic Pearl Street Mall. The red brick, pedestrian-only thoroughfare was colorful, vibrant, and full of life with musicians and jugglers to entertain the walkers and eaters. I took a bunch of pictures to send to Nella and Rosie. When my food arrived, it was beautifully presented, a work of art in its own right. I ate slowly, savoring every bite.

By the time I left, the clouds were clearing and it was time head to campus for the meeting Rachel invited me to.

She was waiting outside the building when I got there, and she led the way to a room that looked like a teacher's lounge. Several women were sitting around a large table; I found a couple of empty seats while Rachel got us some sparkling water from a fridge in the corner.

As more women continued to arrive, it was obvious that most of them knew each other; there was a feeling of warmth and familiarity between them. There were about fifteen women in attendance, mostly middle-aged and professional, when the woman who identified herself as Trish opened the meeting. "Let's open this meeting with a moment of silence, followed by the Serenity Prayer."

Then a woman named Amanda opened the sharing. "Hi, I'm Amanda and I'm an addict. As most of you know, I haven't been back in these rooms for that long. I relapsed when I moved here from California, and I discovered that you people here in Boulder don't know how to run a proper 12-Step Meeting." Everyone laughed. "Everyone knew me at my old meetings; I got clean with those people. When I moved away I tried to find a new sponsor, to no avail, and once again felt like I didn't belong. It brought up so many feelings of anxiety and not fitting in. I relapsed after twelve years of clean time. I only came back because of my ex-husband; he threatened to leave me, said it was either him or the painkillers and booze. I chose him, but it didn't really matter, as you all know he left anyway. But coming back here was the best decision I ever made. When he gave me the ultimatum, I came back to the program after a year of drinking and suicidal thoughts." Amanda had tears in her eyes as she looked around the room. "I'm so grateful I found all of you; you saved my ass." She blew her nose and continued. "But now I'm struggling with a familiar fiend, dealing with powerlessness and control . . . when to let go, and when to fight for what I know is right. I really hate this. I know all about 'let go and let God,' but when I know I'm being screwed, I need to fight."

I felt at right at home. Women talking powerlessness and control, two subjects close to my heart. I sat back and listened.

When Amanda finished speaking, another woman introduced herself. "Hi, I'm Della, and I'm an addict. Shit, Amanda, I can relate. I am going through something similar. I'm in a dispute with the chair of my department, and I want to slit his throat." Many of the women nodded, obviously familiar with the situation. "I've said this many times in this meeting, so this is nothing new to most of you, but I'll repeat it because I need to hear it myself. There are times for the platitudes and bumper stickers of 12-Step slogans, and there are times where I need stronger tools. I'm in therapy again for what this dispute is bringing up for me, and I will probably need a lawyer, goddamn it. 'Let go and let God' will not do it for me here. That monster is trying to get me to leave my position, and he would love me to 'let go,' but I will not give him the satisfaction. This program is so helpful in so many ways, but for some things we've got to access tools available outside these rooms."

I recognized this power struggle. I'd had a similar situation arise at work with a colleague and almost quit my job because of it, but luckily he got transferred to another office before it came to that. I'm always grateful when I hear other women describe problems that I personally have gone through, like I'm not alone trying to manage this messy life.

A third woman stood up and introduced herself: "Hi, I'm Judith, I'm an addict. I hadn't dealt with all my issues when I first came into these rooms; I never knew what I didn't know, until I knew that I didn't know it. And when I first came in, in a small town in northern Colorado, I just did not fit in. There were so many judgmental people in those rooms, so many hurtful and damaging statements, and if I ever said anything negative about the rooms or about 12-Step recovery in general, I was attacked and shamed. So I left, and I didn't come back until I moved down here and met a couple of you. Don't get me wrong, you all know I really respect the steps and what is offered in these rooms; it's the people who screw it up. But in my experience, some people suddenly think they are king and that nothing negative can be said. Many women I know personally have been 'thirteenth stepped' and cannot share what's going on without being attacked. I just do not go to any meetings at all that are coed anymore; I can only handle women's meetings now. I do love the program for the most part; it has absolutely saved my life, yet there are human beings who screw it up for a lot of us. Yeah, yeah, I know 'principles before personalities'—but sometimes the personalities fuck it up for the rest of us. I'm not sure if that fits the topic, but it is what's up for me."

As Judith finished sharing, I thought back to my own experiences with being "thirteenth stepped," the term used when predatory men take advantage of women new to sobriety. I had almost succumbed to one guy, but my sponsor spotted him hitting on me and swooped in and rescued me before it went any further.

"Elsbeth, alcoholic. I've said this before, but it's so relevant . . . I wanted to be free of the consequences of drinking, but not necessarily free of the drink. I just kept thinking I could keep on drinking if I did it differently. It took almost six years in and out of these rooms . . . and in that time I would have sold my soul for a drink. I'm lucky to be alive. What made the difference for me is all of you. I needed the connection, the community . . . the support. I needed you. To me, recovery is about community. I can't do this shit alone."

I decided not to share at this meeting, but to just listen and soak it all in. Several of us went out for frozen yogurt afterward, just as Rachel had promised, and as I walked back to the hotel after my yogurt with fresh raspberries, still basking in the glow of the connection I'd felt that evening, I marveled at how this often happened: that whatever was up for me was often a topic of discussion at a meeting. I thought again about my "patchwork approach," which seemed as relevant as ever.

When I got back up to my room, I pulled out my journal.

*Day Ten and Eleven—Boulder, Colorado*

*I have so much I want to write tonight; I'm just buzzing after an amazing meeting and a wonderful connection to an awesome group of women. I could imagine myself living here in Boulder; I definitely feel a sense of belonging here. I need to thank Rosie again for connecting me to Rachel. She is an absolute font of information. I'm so grateful I got to spend time with her. What a gift!*

*And I realized that although I do need the 12 steps, other tools to aid in my sobriety and growth are essential. A "patchwork approach" is needed; meetings alone aren't enough for me . . . but I don't want to throw the baby out with the bathwater; meetings are vital and provide important community. As one of the wonderful women I met tonight so eloquently put it: "I can't do this shit alone."*

*And added note to self—I have to find more ways to be creative and invite creativity back into my life. After spending some time at the museum today and looking at the colors and the fabrics and array of art on display, I decided I need to get my hands back into it. Creativity connects me back to myself in a way that other things just don't . . . When I get home, I'm signing up for that pottery class I've been meaning to take, pulling out my old easel and paints, and definitely making time to write.*

*Secret? . . . Hmmmmm, well, I didn't really get a "Life's Secret" from anyone, but I learned a lot . . . about trauma and addiction . . . evidence to support what I've known in my bones for so long.*

## CHAPTER 8

# Saying Yes

LINCOLN, NE

---

*"Always say yes to the present moment. Surrender to what is.*
*Say yes to life and see how life suddenly starts working*
*for you rather than against you."*

—ECKHART TOLLE

I was sad to leave Boulder. I had felt such a sense of kinship and belonging there. And I wasn't looking forward to going to Lincoln, Nebraska; it was really just a midpoint between Boulder and Madison. So I lingered over breakfast at the cool café on Pearl Street that Rachel had suggested, enjoying the bright sunshine. But with a seven plus hour drive ahead of me, I needed to get on the road. I took a selfie on the terrace and sent it with a short note to Rosie, thanking her again for her introduction to Rachel, and then walked back to my car. With a heavy heart and a slight sense of foreboding, I got on the road toward I-76 and drove out of town.

With nothing but flat terrain, wide freeway expanses, and the occasional tumbleweed, the drive was so boring that I had to stop twice for coffee just to stay awake. But it offered long expanses of time to reflect. So many of my character defects were playing out in my head on the monotonous journey. I thought back to the myriad ways I had screwed up as a mother. When I had relapsed, I spent far too much time looking forward to my kids going to bed so I could drink undisturbed, and then was only half focused on them in the morning when my head was pounding with a hangover. God, I had wasted so much precious time not being fully present with them. And how many times had I risked their lives after having a few too many glasses of wine and then driving with them in the backseat? I shuddered at the memory. And recent experiences on this trip had brought up so many current flaws like self-criticism, self-sabotage, and so much judgment toward myself and others . . . the list felt never-ending.

It was clear that many of these shortcomings came from experiences growing up: judgement from my dad and insecurity from my mother, both of whom were dealing with their own childhood trauma. When I was triggered and felt unsafe, I withdrew and sought to numb my own pain. The multigenerational aspect of addiction was so obvious and stark. I knew I still had a lot of work to do.

I had booked a room at a budget motel near the university, and when I arrived, there was a big banner outside the motel saying "Home of the Cornhuskers." It did not bode well. A well-fed (corn fed?) dog was lying right in front of the door of the office; I struggled to step over it, carry my bag, and open the door at the same time. When I finally got inside, it was stuffy and hot.

"Sorry, air con is on the blink, and it's so dang hot in here. How can I help, hon?" the woman behind the desk asked, fanning herself with a newspaper.

It was at least ten degrees hotter in the office than it was outside. "Do you want me to open the door to let some air in?" I asked, already sweating.

"Won't help much since there's not even a breath of breeze out there, and then there's those danged mosquitoes gettin' in. Are you Meg?" I nodded. "Yeah, I figured it was you. I booked you in to Room 7, downstairs so you won't have to climb all those stairs, and I made sure the air con was working in there." I picked up a newspaper from the counter and fanned myself while she checked me in. "The room is just over there to the left, first floor. Watch out for Daisy as you're leaving," she said, indicating the dog. "She's old and fat and hates the heat just like her momma."

I slipped the key in my pocket, grabbed my bag, stepped gingerly over Daisy, and made my way to the room.

I had a little time before my meeting was scheduled to start, so I slipped on a sundress and sandals and drove to a nearby restaurant. A pretty, young waitress with a long braid brought me to a corner table. I asked for iced tea and a Caesar salad and looked out the window. The sky was kind of a washed-out blue, and I noticed several contrails. The terrain was flat and uninspiring; I could not imagine living there.

The waitress came back carrying a massive salad and a pitcher of iced tea; she refilled my glass and asked if I needed anything else.

"All set," I said.

"Great. Enjoy!" She flashed me a huge smile.

The salad was really good, cool and crisp. I realized that I had anticipated a subpar salad with limp lettuce. When I was done, the waitress came back, refilled the glass, and left the bill, signed with a happy face next to her name.

I watched her walk away as I pulled out my wallet; I tipped her generously and silently wished her well. *I hope she can get out of this god-forsaken town,* I thought—then immediately chastised myself for being so judgmental. *Perhaps she's happy here.*

The chairperson explained that this was to be a speaker meeting and asked us to please welcome Margaret. I usually didn't like speaker meetings; I found them boring, long-winded, and often whiney. But this was the only women's meeting I had been able to locate, and I was already here, so I stayed.

An older woman stood up and walked to the podium. "Hi, I'm Margaret, and I'm an alcoholic." She cleared her throat and continued, "What it used to be like, what happened, and what it's like now . . . It sounds simple, doesn't it? But getting here was not a straight line, not at all. I'm in my tenth year of sobriety this year. And every year is a learning experience. Let's see, what it used to be like . . . Well, it was a nightmare. I lost my husband, I lost my job, and I lost my self-respect. I kept thinking I could do it on my own, but I couldn't. My world got smaller and smaller; I ended up drinking alone in a small apartment after my husband divorced me and threw me out. One night I drank too much, blacked out, and fell over in the bathroom, cracked my head on the bathtub, and gave myself a concussion. I woke up the next morning alone, with a brutal headache and blood matted in my hair. I took a shower to try to clean myself up a bit and took myself to the hospital. A lovely nurse there suggested AA, and I went to my first AA meeting the next day. I had a great first year of sobriety, a real pink cloud; I figured I was in for smooth sailing . . . but then I met a man."

A few of the women in the room groaned. A few more nodded knowingly.

"Well, I felt strong and thought to myself 'I'm good. I can have a few drinks with this great guy.' And of course, it wasn't long before I was in blackout mode again. He ended up leaving me for a cute little cocktail waitress, and I was back to square one. No, actually not square one; I had taken several steps backward. I ended up back in the same hospital, anemic and malnourished."

Relapse stories always hit me hard; they feel so authentic and real to me since it's what I went through. A knot began to form in my stomach.

"Believe it or not," Margaret continued, "the same nurse found me and looked after me. This time she brought me to the AA meeting herself, as it turns out she was one of us." With these words Margaret smiled at a woman in the front of the room, and her eyes shone with tears. "That was Alice, and she saved my life. She brought me to that meeting that still takes place on Tuesday nights in the cafeteria of the hospital; that was ten years ago, and I haven't looked back since." Margaret blew her nose.

The knot in my stomach tightened as I thought back to the times that I thought that I could have just one or two glasses of wine and ended up emptying the bottle and then finishing off yet another. I can still feel the anguish and remorse of waking up with a pounding head, realizing that I did it again—the shame of feeling powerless and out of control.

"Well, as I said, every year is a learning experience. And this year, my tenth year, is my year of saying *yes!* . . . Yes to everything except drinking and drugging or doing anything illegal. I'm doing as much as I can, as long as I can afford it and as long as I don't hurt others or myself. I read a book that suggested I say yes to life and to whatever presents itself in the present moment—to the good and the bad, not to shy away from the 'bad' stuff." She made air quotes around "bad." "I'm trying not to judge everything, especially myself. I'm trying to accept myself and my life, warts and all. And that is not easy, I promise you that." She paused and took a sip of water. "I'm also trying to say yes to new, and even frightening, experiences. And boy, let me tell you, it's been a wild ride so far. I am saying the word 'yes' in my mind as I approach each new experience, like being the speaker tonight, for example." A few of the women smiled and nodded, acknowledging the courage it takes to stand in front of a room of your peers and tell your story. "Last week I went up in a glider. Now, I gotta tell you, I am terrified of heights and of flying, but a young gal I know is getting her glider's license, and she invited me up; my immediate response was Hell NO!" Margaret paused while the audience laughed. "But I didn't say no. I let myself feel the fear, paused, and then said yes. And it was fantastic . . . terrifying too, but also fantastic." Margaret paused again and looked around the room. "But most importantly, I'm learning to say *yes* to life in that deepest sense. To not push away life in all of its messiness, to embrace all of life. I heard a quote once that said: 'There is something wonderfully bold and liberating about saying *yes* to our entire imperfect and messy life.' That is what I am attempting to do. So I'll close now to say that for so many years, most of my life, I was barely surviving and certainly not thriving. But now I'm thriving, thanks to this program and to all of you. Thank you for being here for me. All of you are keeping me sober today. I encourage each and every one of you to try saying yes to life. Just try it for a week and watch what happens. Thank you."

The applause rang out and vibrated around the room, the love and support was palpable . . . then a dour-looking woman raised her hand and said she'd like to speak. Immediately the energy changed; the room felt flat and wary, as though everyone was anticipating a challenge.

"I'm Janet, alcoholic. Thank you, Margaret, for your share. What I'd like to comment on is when people relapse. Well, I have not re-lapsed, but I know many that do, believe you me, and for women it's usually a relationship that will send them back out . . . not being will-ing to go to any lengths to get well . . . If you want to get well, you need to stay out of relationships, or if you must be in one, only be with someone else in the program, pure and simple. Another reason people relapse is because they are not being honest and they believe lies they tell themselves. People make up lies to avoid doing the work, just like Margaret did, and those lies will get you in trouble. Those lies lead to self-pity, and self-pity is a dangerous thing, and that comes from lack of a spiritual connection. If you want to stay sober, you need to do the work. I've been sober for over twenty years, and I have never relapsed. People relapse from bad choices, bad relation-ships, not going to meetings. You don't go to meetings, you don't do the work, then you suffer the consequences. It's as simple as that." Janet nodded in a self-satisfied way and sat down.

I took a deep breath. This was the sort of chastisement that had driven me away from meetings in the past, and actually led to my own relapse. I wanted to stay to talk to Margaret and thank her for her story, but I also wanted to get away from Janet and her negative told-you-so energy. I considered quietly sneaking out, but I thought of Rachel saying that she learned to take what she needed and leave the rest. But maybe most importantly, I remembered her description of trauma and addiction, and I felt a small wave of compassion gently blooming. I didn't like Janet's words or her tone, but I could imagine her pain, and I softened just a bit.

I stayed until the meeting was over.


I had planned on leaving Nebraska early and just getting out of town as quickly as possible in the morning. But in the morning, I decided to give Lincoln a second chance, a more openhearted approach, and not base my whole experience of the place on my judgmental head. So I got up early, packed my bag, and stopped at the Sunken Gardens before I left town.

The gardens opened at six in the morning, so I was free to enter. The weather was cool, the sky was a deep blue, and the purple, pink, and oranges of the flowers on display in the garden were joyful. I slowed my pace and took time to appreciate the care that went into each area. The different parts of the gardens spoke to me in different ways. The Perennial Garden was shady and full of mauves and purples, and I felt soothed by the colors and the shade. Then in the Annual Garden, I watched volunteers gardening and taking such meticulous care of the plants; they were tended to with such love. I read the plaque that explained that volunteers planted thousands of annuals every year with a different theme each year. I read about one garden a few years ago influenced by Van Gogh's *Starry Night* and thought that would have been amazing to see. And finally I ended up in the Healing Garden with its beautiful white blossoms.

It was calm, serene, and meditative in the Healing Garden. I sat on a bench in the sun and felt a sense of peace wash over me as my heart rate slowed and my breath deepened. I closed my eyes. I felt soft, like my sharp edges blurred just a bit.

By the time I drove out of Lincoln, I had a new appreciation of the city and a renewed focus on keeping my judgement in check. I put on my mix tape and sang my way through Iowa and on to Wisconsin.

I didn't arrive in Madison until well after ten. There was an envelope taped to the door, as promised, where I found the key.

I made my way quietly to the little cabin at the back of the property. Inside, there was a selection of teas, a little electric kettle, and a nice note of welcome. After a warm shower, I sat at the little desk with a cup of tea to write in my journal.

*Day Twelve—Lincoln, Nebraska.*

*Writing from Madison after a long drive from Lincoln. Well, I've passed the midway point and am well and truly on the second half of my journey. Although, there has been much zigzagging, so not really second half in terms of time; with only four more stops and only six or seven more days, I guess I would have to say I'm more than halfway there.*

*So what have I learned? Wow, so much, mostly about me. My old nemesis "judgmentalism" reared its ugly head again. Oy, you'd think I would have learned this one already, especially after all my judgement toward Saskia and how that turned out. This time it wasn't just about a person . . . although I must say there were a couple of people I was not overly fond of, but instead about a place. About Lincoln, Nebraska itself.*

*I drove into town with so much prejudgment. I was judging everyone I met in town just for living there. I couldn't imagine myself living there, so I decided that everyone that did choose to live there was inherently flawed.*

*But after listening to a speaker at a women's meeting there and then going to the Sunken Gardens, I had my eyes—and perhaps my heart—opened a bit. I am making a commitment to myself to be more accepting, less judgmental . . . another patch for my quilt . . .*

*I guess saying yes to life would be the next secret I learned. The speaker at the meeting I went to talked about it, and it made so much sense to me. Not only saying yes to new experiences, which I will absolutely try to do as much as possible, but also accepting life as it is, all of its messiness and imperfections. Learning to say a deep yes to the aliveness that is right here. When I stop comparing myself to others and put away all of those ideas of what life should be like and what I should be like, when I can just accept all of me, then I am free to wholeheartedly and completely say yes to my life as it is. So I want to focus on a new open-mindedness and a willingness to be present to whatever the present brings.*

*Secret #5*

*Yes—saying yes without judging everything.*

## CHAPTER 9

*Forgiveness*

MADISON, WI

_____

> *"By far the strongest poison to the human spirit is the inability to forgive oneself or another person. The challenge is to refine our capacity to love others as well as ourselves and to develop the power of forgiveness."*

—CAROLINE MYSS

I woke up early on my first day in Madison, happy to be back. I had lived in Madison early on in my sobriety and had found a group of amazing women, including a wonderful woman named Tina who had served as my sponsor, while I was there. I was looking forward to meeting up with Tina later that morning and excited to visit one of my favorite haunts, the Saturday Morning Farmers Market in the Capitol Square. I love the vibrancy of the market, the colors, the smells, and the activity.

The Saturday scene on the Square is like attending four activities in one: There's the farmers market itself, with it's beautiful array of produce and flowers and fresh locally produced cheeses and baked goods. Then there's the whole political scene, with its myriad booths giving out information from various non-profit and political organizations. Then there are all the arts and crafts vendors with the eclectic and creative wares. And finally there is always great entertainment from the street musicians and performers.

My Airbnb was walking distance to the square. The walk was nostalgic as I passed places that I had been with my kids. I bought coffee and a cinnamon roll as I arrived and ate it as I meandered around the square. I bought a small bouquet of flowers from one of the stalls I passed, then headed for the café where Tina and I had agreed to meet for coffee—a place I liked just off the square.

I nabbed a table outside and did some people-watching while I waited for Tina. I didn't have to wait long.

"Yay, Meg, there you are," Tina bellowed as she approached. "Ah, aren't you a sight for sore eyes." She walked up and gave me a bear hug.

"Let me get us our coffees before we start catching up," I said. "Be right back!"

When I came back a few minutes later and gave Tina her coffee and the flowers, she stood up and gave me another hug. "Oh, aren't you an angel."

"It is so wonderful to see you. It's been way too long. How have you been?"

Tina took a sip of coffee and recapped the last several years in a concise, upbeat manner that I had missed. When she was done, she leaned forward. "But enough about me. Tell me about this trip you're doing. You called it your 'recovery road trip' in the message you sent me; I love that by the way. I wanna do the same thing; I think everyone I know will want to do one too. I hope you're writing about it as you're travelling."

I sipped my coffee and smiled at Tina over the cup. I loved her enthusiasm. "Yes, I have been writing. My friend, Nella, in Seattle, I'm sure I've told you about her, she gave me a journal before I left Seattle to embark on this journey. But, but . . ." I struggled as I started to recount my journey, words jumbling in my head, and tears sprang to my eyes.

Tina put her hand on mine and smiled, her eyes saying more than words could.

Her compassion and caring was not a surprise, but that soft touch unleashed a current of emotion in me that I was not expecting, and the tears started and soon I was crying in earnest, and the more I tried to stop, the more the crying continued.

"Oh, Meg," Tina said gently. "Just let it come, honey, just let it come until it's done, and then you can talk. I'm right here, just let it come."

I cried in a very unbecoming gulping way until the tears were finished. It always surprises me that if I just let myself cry, without trying to stop it, it ends eventually, even when it feels like it will engulf me.

"Wow, I wasn't expecting that. Sorry."

"You know you never have to apologize for being real with me. Just start talking, let it out, what's underneath those tears."

"I'm not sure. I'm feeling overwhelmed seeing you now, being with someone I care about. I've missed you. And I've had so much time alone on the road trip; it's given me a lot of time for self-reflection, and it's not been very positive. I've been thinking about everything I've done wrong or could have done better. Oh, Tina, I made so many mistakes as a mother. On the drive up here, I was remembering all the time I wasted with my kids when I was either drunk or hungover; I can't get that time back. Now they're grown and gone, and I hate myself for wasting all those years." Tears sprang to my eyes again, threatening to unleash another torrent.

"OK, so I get to remind you about one of my favorite topics . . . self-forgiveness," Tina said, giving me a meaningful look. "We've all fucked up, honey, you know that. But what we learn through our recovery is that forgiving ourselves, not guilt, increases personal accountability. I've said that to you so many times. But it's like that damn onion; layers have to keep coming off until we get to the core. We addicts sure do like to beat ourselves up. We are so good at it."

I smiled at Tina; I loved her wisdom. "Thank you for being here to hold my hand." I blew my nose and took a deep breath. "So let's see, I was going to tell you a bit about the trip. Well, one of the things I've really realized is how much I need to connect to people in recovery. Well, connection to people in general, but to women in recovery in particular."

Tina nodded. "The opposite of addiction isn't sobriety. It's connection."

"Yes! A woman in Boulder quoted that same thing to me—Johann Hari. I love it. But I let myself lose that connection. All that pedantic Big Book thumping made me crazy, so I pulled away, but leaving recovery didn't work either. So that's a big piece of what this trip is about, reconnecting to a healthy recovery and to myself. And another piece is learning people's secrets to life, which I shall ask you about soon, by the way."

Tina took a sip of coffee and waited for me to continue.

"So after talking to these amazing women in Boulder, I decided that what I need is a 'patchwork approach' to my recovery. I need more than just the 12 steps; I need counseling, and to eat well and pay attention to what I am putting in my body and exercise for my body, and to meditate and connect to take care of myself spiritually, and to read nourishing books, and connect with like-minded people.

"Ah, Meg, I love that idea of a patchwork. That reminds me of a concept I heard about just the other day on a podcast I like. Do you ever listen to Podcast Recovery? It's great. It's by two guys in recovery, Eric and David. I don't want to do it an injustice by trying to describe it here, so I'll send you the link when I get home, and you can listen to it. I know you'll enjoy it."

I held my coffee, feeling a little twist in my gut. "Shoot, did they talk about a 'patchwork approach'—damn, I thought I came up with that." I rolled my eyes when I realized how much my ego wanted to take credit for the idea.

Tina smiled. "No, it was called something else, but it was a similar idea. But allow me to change the subject. I want to hear about this secret to life thing you mentioned."

I told her about the dream I had at Nella's house, about asking people about their secret to life, and then asked her to share hers.

She looked out over the square and thought about it for a few minutes. "Hmmmm, well, what's up for me is the conversation we've been having about forgiveness, especially forgiving myself. I mean, we learn all about forgiving others in recovery, and you know my favorite saying by Anne Lamott: 'Not forgiving is like drinking rat poison and then waiting for the rat to die.' But I think the secret that I've learned through the years is that the most important person I have to forgive is myself. I remember my own sponsor used to quote Louise Hay: 'Forgiveness is for yourself because it frees you. It lets you out of that prison you put yourself in.' My sponsor was forever telling me that I was the only one who had the keys to the prison I kept myself in. So yeah, I'd say that is my secret to life, at least for today."

I took a few minutes to let this soak in. Yes, this is what I needed to hear today—my reminder that just because I didn't do it all right, I'm not a complete fuckup. I get to forgive myself for my past mistakes, no matter how badly I judged them to be. Yes, I have to make amends and clean up the mess, but those mistakes don't get to live rent free in my head and beat me relentlessly with a cat-o'-nine-tails.

Tina looked at her phone to check the time. "Damn, I have to go. The morning has just flown by. I'll send that link to the podcast to you; listen to it when you can. And I'll see you tomorrow at the meeting. You will be there, right?"

"Hell yes! I planned my trip to Madison to coincide with that meeting. I wouldn't miss it for the world."

"Fantastic." Tina finished her coffee and gathered up her things. "Thank you again for the flowers, they are just beautiful. And let's plan to get a coffee with some of the other women after the meeting."

"I will." We hugged each other goodbye, and she strode away.

I stayed at the table, sipping sparkling water and people-watching, for another half hour before finally rising and wandering back down State Street.

I drove to the women's meeting the next evening without a problem, on autopilot, even though it had been years since I had been there.

When I went inside, a chorus of greetings rang out—"Meg!" I felt it deep in my bones: I belonged. My defenses melted with each hug, and I cherished the feeling of being held deeply within the community of women I held so dear.

"All right, everyone," called Connie, the meeting chair. "Let's take our seats!"

I went over and sat beside Tina.

Connie read through the familiar opening of the meeting, and the women said the Serenity Prayer together. Then she asked, "Are there any newcomers to the meeting today?"

A young woman tentatively raised her hand. "Hi. I'm Emily," she said quietly. She kept her eyes on her hands clasped on her lap. Her hair was long and stringy and did a good job of hiding her face.

"Hi, Emily. We're glad you're here," the women said in unison.

"Any visitors?" asked Connie.

Several pairs of eyes turned toward me and smiled.

"I'm Meg, and I'm an addict, and I'm so happy to be back here at this meeting."

"Welcome back, Meg," said the room.

"I've asked Joan to do a reading and to open our meeting." Connie yielded the floor to Joan.

"Hi, I'm Joan, and I'm an addict. When Connie asked me to do a reading to open this meeting, I looked around and found this reading online on MindWorks, and it really spoke to me:

'Healing relationships is key to addiction recovery. Finding a way to heal relationships and the pain that can get in their way is core to our recovery. If we're going to move forward towards forgiveness and reconciliation, we must acknowledge the pain and acknowledge the harm and find forgiveness.

Likewise, we acknowledge our own mistakes. When we have self-compassion, when we acknowledge the harm that we have caused others as a result of our own suffering, confusion, greed, and hatred and ask for forgiveness, we find healing.

Forgiveness is the way forward so we don't get stuck in the narrative.

We come together when we can acknowledge what is broken and difficult and hurt within us. It doesn't have to be complicated. Just, 'I forgive myself.' And if I can start to open up space of forgiving myself, it starts to open space for others. If I can be a little softer with myself, I find I can be a little softer with the world.'"

Joan took a breath, looked at the women around the table, and exhaled. "I need to work on forgiveness today. Especially forgiveness for myself because of the way I have treated those people I love. I was an absent mother to my children, a resentful daughter to my parents, and an angry wife to my husband. I burned bridges and blamed everyone near me for how shitty I felt about myself. I drank and took pills to numb my pain. And now I'm dealing with the wreckage of my past. I've been clean and sober a few years now, and I'm just realizing now how much work I still have to do. I'd love to hear from all of you about how you work with forgiveness, for yourself especially, to heal relationships. Thanks."

I shook my head in amazement; there it was again, the very thing I had been thinking about was the topic of the meeting. It was eerie how often this happened.

There was silence for a few beats, and then an older woman spoke up.

"I'm Daisy, and I'm a drunk. Forgiveness is a great topic, thanks, Joan. Beautiful reading, thank you for sharing that. I needed to hear that today. Shit, the wreckage of my past. I've been around these rooms for a few years now, and I still have work to do to clean up my past, and forgiveness is the key. A few of us in here have favorite quotes about forgiveness that I've heard from time to time. Mine is a quote by Miguel Angel Ruiz; I have it up on my fridge." Daisy closed her eyes and recited: "'Forgive yourself. Forgiveness is an act of self-love. When you forgive yourself, self-acceptance begins and self-love grows.'"

Daisy looked around the room. "There's more to it. I don't remember the whole quote, but I've never forgotten that one sentence: forgiveness is an act of self-love. How wonderful is that? Forgiving myself as an act of self-love. Thanks for being here today, ladies. I love each and every one of you."

Several more women shared on the topic of forgiveness, forgiveness of others, but mostly forgiving ourselves for the shit we did when we were in active addiction. But with the very clear reminder that we can't just say "OK, all is forgiven." There is a lot of work to do to truly clean up the wreckage of our past. I remembered my first sponsor saying "amends are action." I had to demonstrate a whole new way of life in recovery; apologies alone were just words. I must align my values to my actions. And with this work came deep healing.

"We have time for about one more share, does anyone have something they want to say before we close?"

Emily looked around shyly and tentatively raised her hand. "Hi, I'm Emily, and I guess I'm an addict. Um, I'm not really sure what I want to say . . ." Emily's voice broke, and a few tears rolled down her face. She took a ragged breath and tried to continue; the other women's silent compassion was tangible. "Um, I just wanted to say thank you. I wasn't sure what to expect when I walked in here. I was scared to come, afraid you were all going to be all holy and judgy and that I wouldn't fit in at all. But my sister told me to come to this meeting; she said it would be a great place to start. And, um, I just want to say thanks; you're all actually amazing. Maybe this isn't such a horrible place, and maybe I can get some help." She finished with a tentative smile.

"Thanks so much, Emily," Connie said. "We are really glad you are here. Would you like a few phone numbers before you go? Most of us are happy to help in any way we can."

Emily nodded, and Connie pulled a piece of paper from a folder next to her.

"According to our seventh tradition, AA is self-supporting through our own contributions," Connie reminded everyone. "I will pass the basket; please give if you can, but remember we need you more than your money. And please add your name and number to the paper for Emily if you're available for support. And I've asked Meg to read the Promises." She smiled in my direction.

As the paper with phone numbers and the basket made its way around the room, I read the Promises, then we all stood together and said the Serenity Prayer. When the meeting was closed, I went around the room hugging these women I had missed so much.

A group of us went out for tea after the meeting, which turned into dinner for several of us. The discussion continued to center on forgiveness but also ventured into meditation and our need for deep connection.

I didn't get home until well after ten. I settled into a comfy soft chair in the corner of the room and opened my journal.

*Day Thirteen, Fourteen, and Fifteen—Madison, Wisconsin*

*I've been on the road for two weeks now, and if I keep to the schedule that Nella and I created, I'm about two thirds of the way through my journey. Only two weeks and I feel like I've learned so much already. Like I've ripped a layer of my skin off and I'm starting to grow a new skin—one that's softer and more supple. Still some very raw patches for sure, but feels so lovely and tender, more vulnerable and open. The wrinkles are still there, though, in abundance . . . but I'm willing to call* those "learning lines" (I heard someone say that at the meeting tonight) . . . lots and lots of learning lines.

I went to my favorite women's meeting today, and the topic was forgiveness, especially self-forgiveness. Ha—of course it was! Amazing how this happens. When I'm focused on something, I hear exactly what I need to hear in a meeting. And what a gift to spend time with Tina. I learn so much every time I'm with her. I remember how I balked when I first learned that I would have to have a sponsor. And now, in retrospect, I am so incredibly grateful for everything I've learned from all my sponsors in the past. My very first sponsor, Nancy, taught me so much. What a treasure.

It's been great being in Madison; I've missed this city a lot. But now it's time to go, heading east. I feel some trepidation now as my journey is ending—only four more stops. But at the same time, I'm feeling an openness and ease that I don't think I have ever felt in my life.

Secret #6

This secret is surely Forgiveness—especially self-forgiveness. A secret I need to keep learning again and again.

## CHAPTER 10

# *Fusion Recovery*

## ANN ARBOR, MI

---

*"Fusion: a union by or as if by melting: such as a merging of diverse, distinct, or separate elements into a unified whole."*
—MERRIAM-WEBSTER'S COLLEGIATE DICTIONARY

I left Madison early the next morning, but before I did, I found the podcast Tina had recommended and downloaded it on my phone. As I drove east, I listened to *Podcast Recovery* and got to know the two podcasters, Eric and David. The more they talked, the more I felt a kinship toward them; it felt like we were old friends. I loved how they described their new idea about recovery. They called it "Fusion Recovery."

They described Fusion Recovery as taking all the important elements from 12-Step recovery that we need to stay healthy and consciously grow, without all the limited thinking involved in some 12-Step rooms. As they spoke, I envisioned how it could work: allowing all addicts to work together, whatever their drug of choice, since it's all addiction. Identifying, practicing, and supporting each other in ways to stay healthy . . . not just abstaining from drinking or using but also adding the important elements needed for a healthy body, mind, and spirit: Eating well and exercising for a healthy body. Reading good books and watching good films to nourish our minds. Setting therapy as needed. And perhaps most importantly for ongoing sobriety, meditating and staying connected to our higher power, whatever that is for each individual, to nourish our spirit. They described it as a whole alchemy, saying, "We like the term 'Fusion Recovery,' because by definition fusion is a union or a merging of diverse, distinct, or separate elements into a unified whole."

As I listened, I felt like someone had taken so many of my recent thoughts about my own recovery and rearranged them and ordered them into a coherent stream. It was alchemy; I loved that.

It was early afternoon when I arrived at Indiana Dunes National Park. I was awestruck by the rugged beauty, like a vast desert next to an ocean. The glacial sands stretched out in every direction.

My heartbeat quickened; I wanted to run up the dunes and roll down the other side like a kid. The sand crunched underfoot like ice chips. The sun was warm, and the breeze off the lake was cool. And there were so many birds. I had no idea what kind of birds they were, but there were a lot of different species, and it was obviously a haven for them.

After exploring the area for about thirty minutes, I headed down to the beach to sit by the water. There were several people at the beach, but it was easy enough to find a secluded spot to have a picnic. I shared my bread roll with various birds, then laid back and fell asleep on the warm sand in the sun.

A sharp ding from my phone shook me from my nap—an audio from Rosie.

She opened her message telling me about the dismal rainy grey winter that New Zealand was experiencing. I felt a small twinge of guilt as I listened with my face tilted toward the sun. She went on to fill me in on bits of gossip from our small town. I finished listening and then recorded an audio response. I told her that Lake Michigan was like an ocean complete with surfers. I mentioned the heavenly sunshine, but I didn't want to rub it in, considering how unhappy she was about the weather back home. Then I told her about the podcast that Tina had told me about and promised to send her the link; I explained how the podcasters had described their perfect recovery as Fusion Recovery—a melting of separate healthy elements that create a unified whole.

As I lay back down on the sand and watched the clouds drift across the sky, I spoke in a stream of consciousness about what I saw as the difference between a patchwork approach and Fusion Recovery— almost like imagining a quilt versus a blender. A quilt has all the patches different and quite distinct, whereas a blender mixes everything together to make the final liquid. Then I signed off and sent the audio.

As I was walking back to my car, a response from Rosie dinged on my phone. I waited until I got to the car to listen. Of course, she loved the idea of Fusion Recovery, as I knew she would. She responded that she could see how it could all blend together in a fluid way, like a dance instead of a static piece.

I sent back a quick response: "A dance instead of a static piece, I love that!" Then I started my car and headed out.


I woke up the next morning in Ann Arbor, a town I'd always been interested in visiting.

I spent the first part of the day exploring the university's campus. The stately buildings made me feel like I was someplace important, more European than American. And the Law Quadrangle looked as though some deity had dropped a piece of Oxford or Harvard in the middle of Michigan.

I had thought that I would just quickly wander through the University but got sidetracked several times by the musicians and chalk artists getting creative on the crisscrossing footpaths. It was already lunchtime by the time I picked up a flyer about the Ann Arbor Farmers Market and realized it was only a short walk away. I strolled through the market, put together a picnic of local delicacies, and sat in the park next to the river to eat.

Once I was settled under a tree overlooking the river, I took a selfie and sent it with an audio to my sons, letting them know where I was and where I was heading. I replayed the audio and listened to my voice as I spoke and realized I sounded stronger and clearer than I had in past audios. I wondered if they could hear it too. Did my voice really sound different, or was that just how I felt inside?

After lunch, I headed to the Matthaei Botanical Gardens and Nichols Arboretum, an easy walk from the park. The gardens were enormous, and the various flowers created an intoxicating fragrance. Although it was late in the season, the peonies were still in bloom. The different shades of pink and lavender reminded me of my childhood room. My mother had been a fan of peonies and pansies, which I remembered calling "clown flowers" as a kid, and my bedroom colors reflected that. I paused and let that soak in; it had been a while since I had a positive memory of my room growing up.

The nature trails were shady and inviting, through forests with the sound of water a constant companion. I made an intentional effort to focus on being in nature, in the present. I thought about what Rosie always said, that her higher power was being in nature, and I could really feel that here. I was also thinking about the fusion approach and decided that the open glade on the trail, by the stream, was the perfect place to meditate. I sat by the stream, putting my feet in the water, and let my eyes gently close and focused on my breath.

With the sun on my back and my feet in the cool stream, I felt light, like I was floating. Time felt stretchy somehow; I had no idea how long I had been sitting there, but when I finally stood up, my heart rate had slowed and my breathing was deeper and more relaxed. I wouldn't say I felt fearless, but I didn't have the aching anxiety that usually lived like a tightly coiled snake in my belly. I was in no hurry to leave, I wanted to relax into and relish the fluidity I felt in my body.

I had brought the Michael Beckwith book in my backpack, so I stayed with my feet in the water and read a bit in the sunshine. I loved reading how Beckwith described *life happening through you*; that felt so right. I felt a bit like a poster child for the book: only a few weeks ago in Seattle, I had felt like a total victim—that life happened to me, that I was a walking example of "Life's a bitch and then you die."

After reading Beckwith's next chapter, that *life happened by me*, I'd decided that I would force a change in my life come hell or high water . . . but that determination had felt false; I'd felt like I was play-acting. Now, reading about relaxing into life, allowing *life to happen through me*, I knew I could allow life to just be, to say yes to life—the difference between feeling like a victim and feeling empowered. It was invigorating and powerful. I took the small notebook out of my bag and took some notes from the book.

When I had finished writing, I turned my face up to the sun and reflected on how I was feeling. My road trip was shaking things up somehow. The path my life was taking had shifted; it was like I had awakened after a long sleep in a different room, in a different town, and the terrain had changed. Vistas seemed to have opened up, and the sky had cleared; it all seemed more spacious, as though I could spread my arms and twirl around without bumping into a bunch of old clutter.

The sun started setting, and it grew shadier and chilly. I packed up my bag and headed back to the hotel. My body was tired and sore from all the walking; a long soak in a bath and a salad for dinner sounded heavenly. I was learning to listen to my body, what to eat and when to rest. *Good Lord*, I thought, *why has this taken so long?*

*Day Sixteen and Seventeen—Ann Arbor, Michigan*

*I've really been enjoying being in nature the past couple of days. The area around the Great Lakes is truly magnificent. I've taken some glorious walks and gotten to know an area of the country I've never had the luxury to spend time in. I haven't spoken to many people, though, and didn't ask anyone about a secret to life . . . but I did learn about something new . . . the whole concept of Fusion Recovery. New in a way, but also a concept that Rosie and I have been talking about for several years. The podcasters Eric and David described Fusion Recovery in a way that really resonated with me. They emphasized all addicts working together, whatever their addiction, because it's all addiction. It feels like the antithesis of the old men in the AA rooms glaring at me and saying: "This room is for alcoholics only. Just don't pick up a drink and come to meetings; you don't need anything else." But I do need so much more than that. And I hated feeling guilty that I needed more than that. It's a whole alchemy. The idea of Fusion Recovery just makes so much sense to me, like a blender mixing it all together. I really liked Rosie's description: it's like a dance instead of a static piece. Perfect!*

*So for today . . .*

*Secret . . . Not really a secret—but a concept—the idea of Fusion Recovery.*

## CHAPTER 11

*Intention*

MORGANTOWN, WV

---

*"Intention determines outcome."*
—OPRAH WINFREY

I got into my car determined to have a playful and interesting day, not just drive to get to Morgantown, sleep, get up, and drive all day to Northampton. So after doing some research, I found out that I could take a slight detour to Sandusky, Ohio, and head to Cedar Point Amusement Park. The drive down and through Toledo was flat and mostly freeway driving, but I had learned to take advantage of this mundane driving time to let experiences percolate a bit.

Today, I was reflecting on my childhood; the memory of my dad singing about a gal in Kalamazoo (I'd stopped there on the way to Ann Arbor and very much liked it) and my mother's passion for flowers in her garden brought a smile to my face and softness in my chest. I had spent so many years remembering my childhood in terms of black and white—telling people that my childhood was horrible and not leaving room for any positive memories. But I was finally ready to accept nuance. It wasn't all one or the other; yes, there was trauma, but there was also love and caring. I took time during the drive to remember little Meg, and I was ready to let that little girl come out to play.

As I approached Sandusky, it became obvious that this was a tourist playground, and as I drove on the Cedar Point Causeway, I noticed all the families with lots of children headed to the theme park. I started to feel a little silly driving in alone, but it was my intention to have some fun in the sun and let loose, so I put my sunglasses on, slipped down in my seat, and drove on.

Cedar Point Amusement Park boasted no fewer than seventeen roller coasters; plenty of slides, and an abundance of water-based experiences, all near the sandy shores of Lake Erie. The last time I had been on a roller coaster was when my boys were quite young, and then I was mostly encouraging them rather than being fully present on the ride. This time I would be on my own and able to feel the thrill of anticipation without the worry of being a mother.

Once inside the park, I stood looking at all the rides, listening to the happy screams of people on the rides, hearing the laughter, and feeling the buzzy energy. I could remember this feeling of anticipation and excitement entering the county fair when I was a kid. I wanted to ride everything at once.

I decided to go on the biggest roller coaster first, the Dragster. As I got in line, I overheard a couple of guys in front of me saying that it only took 3.8 seconds to go from a complete standstill to 120 miles per hour, that the cars ran straight up at a ninety-degree incline, paused at the top, and then raced down.

I looked up at the apex as they described the great views from the top at 420 feet in the air. As I watched the cars race by and loop around, I had serious second thoughts. My inner voice screamed in my head: *No way, this is insane!* and I stepped out of line.

The young me was jumping up and down and wanted to get all whipped around on the ride, while the older, more cautious me was saying hell no, this is crazy. But I thought about Margaret back in Nebraska, whispered *yes* to myself and stepped back into line. The two young guys grinned, patted me on the back, and assured me that it was awesome.

Then it was my turn to get buckled in. I could feel the anticipation of everyone on the ride before we started moving; people were looking around more frantically and there was a slightly hysterical edge to the conversations around me. I was hyperventilating and my hands were shaking. My heartbeat was pounding in my chest like a Japanese Taiko Drum. The cars jolted as they started the ascent, and I thought I was going to pass out . . . but as soon as the cars reached the apex and started racing down and circling around, I started laughing uncontrollably. It was like I was ten years old again, feeling the thrill of being out of control. This was a whole different "out of control" than the drunken kind; this was fast and fun but ultimately safe.

I stayed at the park for over four hours and went on every roller coaster there. I had to restrain myself from literally running to the next ride. And there were so many waterslides. Steep slides going straight down where I thought I would fly off my rubber mat, corkscrew slides that left me struggling to stand up when I got to the bottom, and several that combined speed and loops that left me so dizzy I had to sit down after the ride. The description of "kid in a candy shop" didn't come close to describing the thrill and electric buzz coursing through my body.

By the time I left, my hair was wet, my skin was burned, and my stomach was empty—but I felt amazing.

I found a small restaurant right on the water with nice outside seating for dinner. Their specialty was pizza, and the smell of pies in the oven made my stomach growl so loudly that the couple at the next table turned around and smiled.

I cringed, feeling embarrassed, then we all started laughing

When the pizza finally arrived, I ate so quickly that I burned my mouth and had to wait a few minutes and drink some water until I could resume eating. While I waited, I took out my phone and called Nella.

"Meg, yay! I've been hoping to hear from you. How are you? Where are you?"

I updated Nella about the trip, told her about having fun at the amusement park and about saying yes to new experiences. When Nella asked about other new secrets, I told her about Madison and my thoughts about forgiveness.

"You sound different," she said in a thoughtful tone when I'd finished telling her everything. "I can't put my finger on exactly how, but you sound clearer and stronger somehow."

Her words affirmed what I had been feeling for the last few days. "Thank you for noticing," I said, feeling a little emotional. "I *feel* those things!"

I really felt like I had grown so much in various ways on this journey, it felt important to be heard, to be seen. "Nella, it's hard to explain the changes I've gone through, but this trip has been so intense, it feels like I've changed in so many intricate ways, and you saying that you can hear it in my words and in my voice means a lot to me."

"You sound more centered, Meg, stronger, more sure of yourself somehow. It's hard to put my finger on, but it's resonating, I can feel the difference in my own body."

By the time I arrived in Morgantown, it was getting dark, and I was exhausted. The main thing that I noticed as I drove into the city was the river that dominated it. The Monongahela River wound through the town and seemed to be one of the main features of the city, that and the historic brick buildings. It looked like it would be a fun place to explore with the walking trails by the river and the Spark Imagination and Science Center nearby, but at that particular moment, all I wanted to explore was a comfortable place to lie down.

I found the Airbnb easily and walked slowly up to the porch. The door was answered almost as soon as I knocked. A youngish, very fit-looking woman answered the door with a bright smile. I felt very old and tired.

"You must be Meg. Welcome!" she said as she opened the door. "Here, let me help you with your bag; you look exhausted. I'm Candice, my mom owns this property, but I live here and manage it for her. Here, just follow me down the hall to your room."

I struggled to keep up with her as she bounced ahead. Negative thoughts of Saskia in Taos popped into my head as I remembered being bombarded with her chatter on arrival, following her down the hall. I chastised myself for my negativity as I remembered how kind Saskia had turned out to be. But I was tired and not as open-minded as I could have been.

"Here is your room, and there is a bathtub here in the bathroom if you need a soak." She paused and took in my undoubtedly disheveled appearance. "Long day?"

"Actually, yes." I nodded. "I'm exhausted. I stopped at the amusement park in Sandusky on my way here and well, it's just been a long day and a long drive."

"Wow, cool," she said. "I've heard they have awesome roller coasters there. My boyfriend went there a couple of years ago."

"Yes, that's true. It was a fun spot." After her comment about her boyfriend and the roller coasters, I looked more closely at Candice. When I realized she was barely older than my sons, I softened a bit. "And yes, thank you, a soak in a bath sounds divine."

"I'll get you some bath salts and a candle; that should help," Candice said as she skipped out the door. Again, the similarities to Saskia popped into my head, but in a positive way, remembering how healing my time in Taos turned out to be. I looked around the pale-yellow room, with flowers on the table, grateful to be there.

As Candice came back into the room, she tilted her head and asked: "Do you do yoga? I'm going to yoga in the morning before my class; I'm a grad student at the university here. Do you want to join me? The instructor is amazing, and it's early, so you can get on the road and out of town in plenty of time."

I was about to refuse, but a voice in my head reminded me to say yes. "Oh, my goodness, I haven't done yoga in years, I don't know that I'll be able to do it . . . but I think it would be great for my body, so I'll say a tentative yes, OK? Let's see how I feel in the morning, but for now, my body is urging me to crawl into that bath."

"I'll be in the kitchen, ready to make you some breakfast anytime between six thirty and seven fifteen, but if you decide to sleep in, I'll leave food on the counter," she said before quietly shutting the door behind her.

I went into the bathroom, turned on the tap, and liberally poured in bath salts. When the tub was full, I lit a candle and slipped in. As I stretched out in the water, I let out an audible sigh.


I felt a bit groggy when I got up at six thirty. I splashed my face, brushed my teeth, and went down the hall to find the kitchen. I entered a sunny, brightly painted room and saw Candice wearing leggings and a tiny top, showing off a flat, tan stomach.

I looked down at my baggy shorts and T-shirt and rolled my eyes. *I'm not going to yoga to impress anyone*, I told myself. *I'm just going to stretch my body before a long drive.*

Candice looked up from cutting fruit and smiled. "I'm making a smoothie for myself. Would you like some eggs? Toast? Cereal?"

"Actually, Candice, I would love a smoothie, that sounds perfect. But first I need a coffee."

"Of course. Coffee is made and over in the pot on the counter. There are cups over there and milk and sugar too. Help yourself while I finish making the smoothies."

"Great, thanks." I got some coffee and sat down as Candice blended our breakfast.

"I'm so glad you decided to join me at yoga," she enthused over the roar of the blender. "Our teacher is amazing. She is so knowledgeable and focused, and she does the most awesome Savasana at the end of each session."

"Savasana?" I asked. I vaguely remembered the term from decades ago when I had done some yoga, but I couldn't recall what it meant.

"Sorry." She giggled. "My mother tells me that I throw certain words around like they are common vernacular. Savasana, or Corpse Pose, is when we lay quietly on our backs in relaxation at the end of a session. Sonny, our teacher, uses beautiful music and lavender-scented eye pillows. It's fantastic."

"Oh, that does sound wonderful," I said. "But to be honest, I'm a bit worried about going with you. I know it will be good for me, but you are so young and obviously so fit, I know I won't be able to keep up with you. And I don't have a yoga mat or anything."

"Oh, don't worry about the gear, there are plenty of mats and equipment at the studio," she said. "And please don't worry about keeping up with anyone. There are about twenty people that come regularly to this morning's practice, and we vary in age from about twenty to about eighty, and everyone moves at their own speed. There's one woman who is probably in her midseventies who spends half the class in child's pose and does a modified version of almost every pose."

*Midseventies?* I thought. *That's more like it!*

"I'll introduce you to Sonny, our instructor, when we arrive, and you can tell her that you haven't done yoga in a while and let her know if you have any sore bits," Candice said kindly.

"Well, that's a relief!" I said with a laugh. "I honestly was picturing myself in a room with a bunch of young nubile women, twisting themselves in knots while I lay on the floor like a beached whale."

"It'll be fun," Candice said. "I promise."

———

The yoga studio was located on the outskirts of town, about ten minutes away from the Airbnb. When I followed Candice into the yoga studio, there was soft music playing, the light was subdued, and there was a soft subtle fragrance throughout. There were ten or so women, laying on their backs or doing gentle stretches as we set up our mats. Candice motioned to me to come over to front of the room to meet the instructor.

"Meg, this is Sonny. Sonny, this is Meg." She introduced us in a low voice. "Meg is a guest at my mom's Airbnb, and she looked like her body could use a bit of yoga when she came in last night."

"Candice, I should pay you a finder's fee for all the women you bring to this class." Sonny focused her radiant smile on me and held out her hand. "Hi, Meg, so glad you could attend. Anything you'd like to share about pain or injuries that different postures could impact? I really emphasize that every practitioner should move at her own pace, but it's helpful to know if I should be aware of anything."

"No, nothing in particular," I said. "Just a tight, sore body from driving across country. I started in Seattle a couple of weeks ago and have been driving quite a bit almost every day."

"Oh wow, that sounds like an adventure," Sonny said, eyes wide. "Where are you headed next?"

"I'm on my way to Northampton, Massachusetts, today, then on to Boston after that; a coast-to-coast journey."

"Oh!" She looked delighted. "If I may, I have a suggestion for a stop on the way to Northampton today; I know it's a long drive, but you'll have a rare opportunity for a wonderful experience along the way. Can you stay a couple of minutes after class today and I'll tell you more?"

"Oh, I'm intrigued," I said, my curiosity piqued. "I will absolutely stay to hear more about it."

Sonny smiled and started to greet the class as Candice and I made our way back to our mats.

——

After a glorious hour of gentle stretching and a full relaxation at the end, complete with lavender-scented eye pillows as promised, Candice and I said goodbye, and I waited for Sonny to finish rolling up her mat and join me in the back of the room by the door.

"So glad you could stay for a few minutes," she said. "I think a stop at Kripalu Center for Yoga and Health would be well worth your while. It's on your way, just a very slight detour. It's one of my favorite places in the entire country."

"Wow, um, that sounds wonderful," I said awkwardly, "but what is—what did you call it? Kripooloo? And where is it?"

"Sorry, let me back up." Sonny laughed. "Kripalu is a yoga and meditation center located in Stockbridge, Massachusetts. The center teaches yoga and mindfulness and much more. They inspire people to experience yoga as more than just poses and stretches, instead to use it as a practice that inspires connection, compassion, and joy. They have classes and retreats and often have teachers come to speak. And tonight Tara Brach is speaking. I think she's doing a retreat for the weekend, but tonight she is giving a free talk and meditation practice. If I was passing through, I would certainly make it my intention to attend."

I couldn't believe my luck. "Oh my God! I love Tara Brach—she's one of my favorite teachers. That sounds amazing. Thank you so much for everything, Sonny. Your class is just what my body needed, and I'm so excited to get the chance to go to this center."

Sonny gave me a hug and turned to finish cleaning up after the class, and I went down to my car to set the GPS for its new destination.

It was a long drive to Stockbridge, but the podcasts and music had helped pass the time. I smiled and silently thanked Nella one more time as I put on "Sweet Baby James" by James Taylor midway through the journey; I had never known where Stockbridge was, and now I too was going to be on my way from Stockbridge to Boston.

I found Kripalu Center, got out, and stretched. The grounds were so green, almost iridescent. Leafy trees surrounded the grassy expanse near the building with a lake in the distance. I wanted to lie down on the grass and just take in the beauty, but instead I walked up to what looked like an entrance and found a sign about programs planned for the evening. As luck would have it, there was a yoga class starting soon, leaving just enough time to get a bite to eat before the talk by Tara. Yoga twice in one day was a first, but I was grateful for the opportunity.

I was able to sign up for the class and pay the nominal fee for the hour-long session. The teacher was welcoming and the practice, although more strenuous than Sonny's class had been, was still doable, and I didn't feel too out of my depth.

At the end of the class, during Savasana, the instructor spoke about intention.

"Thank you all for taking the time in your busy schedules today to make yoga practice a priority. During this evening's Savasana time, I'd like to speak a bit about intention. As many of you know, I consider making intentions each day to be incredibly important. As one of the world's great teachers, Deepak Chopra explains, 'Intention is the starting point of every dream. It is the creative power that fulfills all of our desires and needs.' I believe that everything that happens to us begins with intention. Our wisest teachers have observed and taught that our destiny is ultimately shaped by our deepest intentions and desires. The Upanishads declares: 'You are what your deepest desire is. As your desire is, so is your intention. As your intention is, so is your will. As your will is, so is your deed. As your deed is, so is your destiny.' Deepak Chopra invites us to 'Slip into the Gap' while we set our intentions, and what better way to do this than during Savasana; this is the ideal time to plant the seeds for intention, while your awareness remains centered in the quiet field of all possibilities. Feel the deep contentment and peacefulness of this relaxed state; intention is much more powerful when it comes from a place of deep contentment. Trust that all will unfold beautifully as you release it into the 'fertile ground of pure potentiality' as Deepak puts it."

While music played in the background, I contemplated the idea of intention. When I thought of the image of a "fertile ground," I pictured myself lying like a starfish in that grassy meadow outside with the view of the lake, the intention of contentment and peace pulsating around me as I fully opened myself up, arching my back, lifting my heart. I felt a gentle smile spreading across my face and the ever-present tension around my eyes melting away.

After a few minutes, the teacher gently brought us back from our reveries. "So as we end our time in Savasana, I'd like to invite you all to make an intention before rising and going out in the world again. Take this opportunity, while you are quiet, relaxed, and in 'The Gap,' to set an intention for the rest of this evening, for tomorrow, and into the future."

As I lay there, I decided that my intention would be to keep growing on this path that I found myself on; to keep learning new pieces that would lead to feeling more fulfilled and peaceful in my own life. In my mind's eye, I pictured it like a lotus flower unfurling, opening to the fullness of what life could be.


After leaving the yoga class, I explored the grounds until I found the café. The buffet table was a treat for the senses—a colorful array of fresh fruits and vegetables, tempeh and tofu and rich green leafy salads, with the smell of freshly baked bread wafting throughout. My mouth was watering before I even picked up my plate to make my selections. Everything was presented beautifully with hand-thrown pottery bowls and fresh flowers on all the tables.

I helped myself to some tempeh, vegetables, brown rice, fresh-baked warm bread, and a small salad. It all looked so fresh and inviting; I wished that I had eaten like this from the beginning of the trip. I was reminded again about Fusion Recovery, that what I put into my body impacts my whole being deeply. I ate slowly and contemplated all the ideas swirling around in my head. Recovery was so much more than just "plugging the jug" as some old-timers put it. Yoga was certainly now on my list of things that lead to a healthy recovery. The list was growing longer by the day.

A soft bell rang.

"Anyone planning to attend the meditation and talk by Tara Brach this evening should now make their way to the main hall," a woman announced.

What I'd come here for! I couldn't wait to hear what Brach had to say.


I was so excited when Tara Brach stepped onto the stage in the meeting hall; I had read so many of her books and listened to so many of her talks that to be in her presence was like being at a rock concert. Like a giddy fan, my heart rate accelerated, and I craned my neck to get the best view. Tara greeted the audience with her brilliant smile and began the talk with one of her stories:

"I'm so happy to see all of you here. I was talking to a woman before I came in; it's her first time at Kripalu, and she got lost on her way here, and that reminded me of one of my favorite stories about getting lost . . .

A gentleman who played the bagpipes was asked by a funeral director to play at a graveside service for a homeless man. The dead man had no family or friends, so the service was to be held at a pauper's cemetery in an area that the gentleman had never been, and he got lost. When he finally arrived about an hour late, he saw that the funeral director had evidently left and the hearse was nowhere in sight. There were only the diggers and crew left and they were eating lunch. The gentleman felt badly and apologized to the men for being late. He went to the side of the grave and looked down, and the vault lid was already in place. He felt so guilty and didn't know what else to do, so he started to play his bagpipes. The workers put down their lunches and began to gather around. He played his heart out for this homeless man who had been buried with no family and friends. And as he played 'Amazing Grace,' the workers began to weep. They wept, then the gentleman wept, and they all wept together. When he finally finished and had packed up his bagpipes and started walking back toward his car, he heard one of the workers say, 'Sweet mother of Jesus, I have never seen anything like that before, and I've been putting in septic tanks for over twenty years.'"

We all laughed and were all fully captivated as Tara continued.

"My dharma talk tonight centers on listening to our deepest intentions. One of the most powerful spiritual practices in the world is to reflect on your heart's deepest intention. There is a vast difference between ego-based intentions that perpetuate thoughts, feelings, and actions that keep us imprisoned in feeling separate and limited, as opposed to remembering our deeper intentions, which call us home to the freedom of our true nature. This is the practice of mindfulness of intention. When you become aware of intention before you act, you are able to make wise choices that lead you to clarity, well-being, and harmony. Think about it; you can do the very same act, and do it out of resentment or frustration, with the intention to just get it over with, or it can be done with the desire to be present, to connect in a caring or loving way. These two ways of doing the same act produce very different results. Whenever you become mindful of your intentions, you have greater freedom to decide how you want to act. Your intentions have a powerful impact on others, and these intentions help to shape their response in turn. This is why it is so valuable to mindfully pause; always take a breath and check in with your intention before you act."

That made so much sense to me, taking a mindful pause and checking in with myself, creating the freedom to decide how I want to act. So much of my life, I felt like I was that little steel ball in a pin-ball machine, bouncing off of things and changing direction, only to be flipped in another direction with no apparent agency in the matter.

After the dharma talk, Tara took questions, and finally the evening concluded with a twenty-minute meditation. Everyone shuffled around for a few minutes, getting into a comfortable position for the meditation, and then Tara led us in a breathing exercise and a body scan, then it was silent.

After I had been sitting silently for a few minutes, my ears started buzzing and I had a strange sensation of my body slowly revolving. Then as the moving sensation stopped, I had the bizarre feeling that my body was expanding, growing larger and larger; my hands felt immense, my head felt like it was inflating like a balloon. The odd sensations didn't really frighten me; I was more intrigued and honored than scared. It felt distinctly like a spiritual experience. My body seemed to be as large as the room, but instead of pushing everyone out of the room, everyone seemed to become part of me as I expanded. The moment seemed to last forever, and yet at the same time was over far too quickly; Tara rang a soft bell to bring us back from the meditation, and the moment was gone as quickly as it had come.

I sat very still, trying to hold on to the magical feeling that I had experienced. After a few more minutes of stillness, I got up slowly and exited the hall.

I walked back to the car in a state of awe. The experience during meditation felt like a confirmation that the events of the past few days had indeed been leading to a transformation of sorts, like I had walked through a portal and was now entering a new realm. It was as if each experience I had had on the journey so far was a twist in the Rubik's Cube, getting everything lined up just right.

I thought back to the coincidence of events. The chance yoga class in Morgantown that led to me to Kripalu Center, arriving just in time for another yoga class and a meditation on intention, and finally a talk by Tara Brach again on intentions, culminating in my amazing experience during the meditation. I had to believe the old adage, "There are no mistakes in the universe."

By the time I arrived at my Airbnb in Northampton, it was almost 11:00 p.m. There was an envelope with my name on it with the key inside taped to the door of the little studio in the backyard. I quietly went inside and made myself a cup of chamomile tea. I took a shower and stretched out on the comfy bed under the skylight, and then I took out my phone to leave an audio message for Rosie.

"Hello, my friend. I've been thinking about you a lot today. Right now, I'm lying on my back on my king-size bed in my Airbnb in Northampton, and I'm looking up through a skylight at the big dipper from my bed. How cool is that? Oh, Rosie, it's been an amazing few days. Remember the last time I left you an audio about that podcast and the concept of Fusion Recovery? I sent you the link; I hope you have had a chance to listen to it. I've had so many wonderful coincidences on this trip; it's been amazing . . . ha . . . I can just hear your voice in my head telling me that 'coincidence is God's way of remaining anonymous.' Anyway I wanted to send this audio tonight to remind us to set an intention to start our own meeting when I get home, a meeting that welcomes all addicts, of any substance or behavior, and that focuses on this concept of Fusion Recovery, focusing on becoming the best version of ourselves, nurturing ourselves, putting healthy food in our bodies, exercising, doing yoga perhaps, reading uplifting books, doing therapy when needed, etc. Reminding people that sobriety is so much more than 'pluggin' the jug' as those horrible old men used to tell us. And on that note, I must send this audio and then take a minute to write in my journal before nodding off to sleep. It's almost midnight and I am exhausted. I love you and I promise to call once I reach Boston."

I got up and shut the window in the little cottage and had one last pee before I went to sleep. I turned on the little bedside lamp, leaned back on the headboard, and took out my journal and trusty purple pen.

> *Day Eighteen and Nineteen—Morgantown, West Virginia, and arriving in Northampton, Massachusetts, with a stopover at Kripalu Center for Yoga and Health*
>
> *Wow, what a full two days. I'm so exhausted but energized at the same time. I've been practicing what I've been learning, and I said yes to a day of play. It was a blast, I felt like such a kid. I said yes to just having fun without feeling guilty about it. I was also reminded today that I really enjoy doing yoga, it feeds my body and soul. Then I had the most amazing opportunity to visit Kripalu Retreat Center, and attend a dharma talk and meditation by none-other than the incredible Tara Brach! I don't know how to describe the experience I had doing meditation with her. It honestly was a spiritual experience . . . At the risk of hyperbole, I feel changed, elevated somehow—my body feels looser, as if a tightly sprung coil has been allowed to release into a loose spiral, like a fern unfurling.*
>
> *And Brach's dharma talk was about intention; that impacted me deeply. Setting the intention, at the beginning of this road trip, to explore and uncover secrets of life, has put me on a journey I could never have imagined. I am reminded of the old adage—"When the student is ready, the teacher appears."*
>
> *My life is a miracle that just keeps unfolding. And now to bed . . .*
>
> *So for today . . .*
>
> *Secret #7*
>
> *Intention—mindful, deepest intention in all I do.*

# *Gratitude*

### NORTHAMPTON, MA

*"The movement of grace toward gratitude brings us from the package of self-obsessed madness to a spiritual awakening. Gratitude is peace."*

—ANNE LAMOTT

T he light of dawn gently peeking in through the skylight woke me up at about six thirty. I stretched languidly, in no hurry to jump out of bed. It felt good to have nothing on my schedule, no long drive or list of things to see. I did a short meditation in bed and set my intention for the day before I got up—all part of my Fusion Recovery plan.

I got up and made a cup of tea, and while it steeped, I did some gentle stretches on the floor. There was a platter of fruit, some muesli, and milk on the little counter in the kitchenette. I sat by the window and ate while I decided what to do. I knew the Forbes Library was nearby, so I thought I'd walk in that direction and find coffee near the Smith College campus along the way.

As I was walking, I watched the way the sun shone through the myriad trees bordering the campus. A gentle breeze moved the leaves slightly and diffused the light in a beautiful way. I kept stopping, mesmerized by the play of light, so when a student bumped into me on the sidewalk not anticipating my sudden stop, I decided I'd better find coffee and sit down to watch.

I found a small café nearby, ordered a coffee, and just watched the light show. I wondered if the light was different here, or if I had just never taken the time to notice. Time felt different somehow, more stretchy and flexible. I wasn't sure if it was because I wasn't in a hurry to get somewhere or see something, or if it was all part of the transformation that I had been going through. I thought back to Saskia and her cleansing, and the serendipitous experience of yoga and Tara Brach's talk. It wasn't just the light that I was experiencing differently. I really felt like I was experiencing life differently; I was seeing things more crisply, like I had removed some Vaseline off of my glasses, and the breeze felt like it was tickling my skin in a way that I had never felt before.

After finishing the coffee, I slowly made my way to the Forbes Library. The library, or the Castle on the Hill as it is sometimes referred to, is a glorious old building completed in 1894, an architectural piece of art; it reminded me of something out of an old movie with Katharine Hepburn. And how wonderful that it is Northampton's public library, open to everyone. I went in, not sure what I was looking for, but felt somehow confident that I would find what I needed to know.

As I approached the desk just inside the main entrance, I saw a sign hanging on the wall just behind the librarian that said: 'I don't have to chase extraordinary moments to find happiness—it's right in front of me if I'm paying attention and practicing gratitude.'—Brené Brown."

"Oh my goodness, I just love that quote," I said to no one in particular.

"I'm so glad. I just put it up this morning," replied the librarian from behind the counter.

"It is exactly what I needed to see today. I feel like you put that up for me to see right this moment." I realized that I had tears in my eyes, but made no attempt to hide them, feeling like it was the exact right response. "I think gratitude is the final piece . . . I'm not even sure I know what I mean by that."

"Well, it makes perfect sense to me." The librarian smiled. "I'm Joy by the way."

"Your name suits you," I said as I smiled at her. "I'm Meg." I looked over my shoulder to make sure that there was no one else waiting for the librarian's attention. "Do you have a couple of minutes? I'd love to talk to you about that quote and ask you a few questions."

"Of course! That is what I am here for; it's my job, isn't that great? Let's go over to that table over there, and I'll just tell Annie to take over the counter for a few minutes." Joy picked up her water bottle and walked over to join me.

Before she came over, I looked at the myriad books in the corner by the table. Several titles jumped out at me, and I was looking forward to exploring more fully after I talked to Joy. As she approached the table, I sat down, eager to learn whatever she could share with me. That simple quote by Brené Brown had given me tingles and caused my stomach to do a few somersaults, and I had learned on this trip to trust it when my body spoke to me. There was a piece of the puzzle in my life's lesson search that I was going to learn from Joy—I could just feel it.

When she sat down, I asked her about her background and what led her to put up that quote this morning.

"I try to put up a new quote every few days to somehow inspire people that come in; I just listened to one of Brown's podcasts last night, and she talked a lot about gratitude, and that quote just felt like it was the one for today. Your response tells me that I was right." She smiled and nodded her head in a job-well-done way.

She asked me about why I was in Northampton, and there was something about her that felt so empathetic and caring that I found myself opening up to her—about my father, the road trip, the past judgements I had had, not only about other people, but especially about myself.

"Oh wow, TMI, huh?" I said, blushing, when I realized how long I'd been talking.

"No not at all, Meg, I'm honored that you shared this with me. Thank you."

"I've been looking for answers on this trip, and I don't know, it just feels like that one quote by Brené Brown solidifies so many things that I've been learning and trying to put together. It feels like I need gratitude to connect it all together somehow, that it creates that fulfillment and depth I've been searching for, if that makes sense."

I was wondering if once again I was dumping on a total stranger. I could feel a blush creeping up as the heat reached my cheeks. I looked down, about to apologize for my oversharing, when Joy touched my arm.

"Actually, that makes perfect sense. I think of gratitude as one of the keystones that helps us evolve to a higher state. Research has shown that it is one of the most effective ways to grow and build a more positive and resilient brain." Joy paused and sipped her water. "This is my passion if you haven't already picked that up." She smiled and tilted her head as she looked at me. "I'm not sure what you wanted to ask me about, but I can definitely share some of the research and why I know that practicing gratitude will change your life."

"Oh yes, please, this feels exactly right. I made the intention this morning to be more present with whatever today might bring, to be open and to hear what I needed to learn today. So please share your knowledge with me; I am all ears." I could tell that Joy was exactly the person I needed to talk to at this point in my journey.

"There is a wonderful professor of psychology at the University of California, Davis, named Robert Emmons. He is the world's leading scientific expert on gratitude. He has done outstanding research on the subject and is just a wonderful man. I've had the good fortune of listening to him speak on several occasions. Emmons explains that when we are in a state of gratitude, we become more expansive and open; we tend to feel lighter, happier, and more content. In this state, we are cultivating more positive relationships, with ourselves and with life in general. It not only changes our feeling in the moment, but it can actually change our brain's chemistry; it can alter our entire relationship to the world."

I stood up and put my bag on my chair and riffled through the contents. "Do you mind if I take some notes?" I asked as I pulled out my notebook. "I don't want to forget any of this. And I'd love it if you could recommend some books for me too." The somersaults that my stomach had been doing now turned to major acrobatics. I felt as if I was being presented with such important information, I didn't want to miss anything.

"Oh, I can definitely do that." Joy sat back and crossed her legs, comfortably; I could tell she was in her element. "There are a couple of great TED Talks as well. Another wonderful expert on this topic is a neuroscientist named Dr. Rick Hanson. His research shows us that gratitude overrides our negativity bias. Are you familiar with that term—negativity bias?"

I shook my head no.

"Negativity bias is the idea that the human psyche is more affected by negative things than by those that are positive. The effect of the negativity bias is that even if positive things are happening around you, the negative things usually dominate your thinking and emotions. Hanson explains that the human brain has a natural negativity bias to internalize negative experiences more deeply than positive ones. According to Dr. Hanson, the brain is like Velcro for negative experiences and Teflon for positive ones. Isn't that a great descriptor?"

I had a picture in my mind of me standing behind a Teflon shield looking out, with all the kind words ever said to me dripping off it before they ever had a chance to reach me. But behind me, I saw the back of my head with dark prickly mean words stuck to my Velcro hair. It was not a pretty sight.

Joy continued, "Our brains are hardwired to remember negative experiences and quickly forget positive experiences. Think about it, Meg, for example, if you go to a party, and maybe four friends tell you that you look wonderful, but one person makes a negative comment about what you're wearing, or how your hair looks; which comment will you remember all night?"

"Oh boy, that's for sure." I grimaced. "And if I looked in the mirror and thought I didn't look all that hot to begin with, it's like that statement is shouted at me through a megaphone," I said as I wrote down Dr. Hanson and underlined the term negativity bias.

"Exactly. Well, there is actually an evolutionary reason for that bias. In the old days, the brain operated that way to alert us to possible danger; if we had to be aware of wild animals about to strike at any minute, we didn't have time to stop and admire the flowers in a meadow. We needed to be looking over our shoulder, hypervigilant about any impending danger, so we developed negativity bias and thus negative things become a magnet for our attention."

I nodded; it made perfect sense to me. "But how does gratitude change that? I mean, I understand what you're saying about the negativity bias, and I've certainly experienced that firsthand, but how does gratitude disrupt that cycle?"

Joy got up, scanned a shelf to our left, lifted a book from it, and put it on the table as she responded: "That is an excellent question, Meg. Psychologists who study the negativity bias have established that each day up to 80 percent of our thoughts are negative, so that is a lot to overcome. Research has shown that when we practice gratitude consistently, we are interrupting that negativity bias. Positive experiences have to be focused on deliberately and consciously in order for them to really sink in. We have to really focus and choose to look for the positive."

I wondered if people really did this. I didn't think I knew anyone who did. We were all too busy getting our important chores done. I barely noticed positive experiences; it was more that I was relieved that I had avoided the many potential catastrophes in my path.

"Research has shown that it takes five positive interactions to make up for a single negative interaction in a relationship, and then it's been shown that to really absorb a positive experience, you need to focus on it for at least fifteen seconds. So we have to learn to pause, to take the time to let the positive sink in, and then to express gratitude about that positive encounter." Joy paused and took another sip of water and smiled at me. "So if you see a beautiful sunset tonight, pause, take the time to appreciate it, and feel a sense of gratitude for your eyes that see it, for the world that produced it. And if someone says something nice to you, pause, allow it to really sink in, and say thank you. Smiling or simply saying thank you to someone can reduce the negativity bias."

I thought of all the times that I was too preoccupied to appreciate a sunset or a beautiful flower, that I had way too many more important things to do. And, with a twinge of sadness, I reflected on all the times that different people had said something kind to me or complimented me in some way, and instead of saying thank you, I brushed it off and doubted their sincerity.

"By expressing gratitude," Joy went on, "we are focusing on the good that exists, thus overriding the negative. In the brain, it's been shown that a smile stimulates the 'feel good' hormone called oxytocin, thus strengthening positivity. We are always strengthening something, so we can just fumble along and continue doing what we've always done since the days of the saber-toothed tiger, or we can cultivate gratitude and appreciate what is good in our life and thus help our brains evolve."

I looked up from my notebook, trying to write as fast as I could.

Joy smiled. "The book I just took from the shelf is *Gratitude Works* by Robert Emmons. It is a great resource and a wonderful guide for cultivating gratitude as a way of life. And I'll write down the names of a few more books and talks online." She looked over at the desk and saw that a few people were waiting for Annie. "Well, looks like I need to get back to work behind the counter at the moment, but do come over before you leave when it quiets down a bit, and I'll give you that list I promised."

"Oh, absolutely," I said quickly. "Sorry I monopolized your attention for so long."

"My pleasure. This is my favorite part of the job. By the way, if you're going to stay here for a while, go over to the shelves where I just got that book and you'll find a lot of information about what we've been talking about." She indicated the area that I had been perusing before we sat down.

As Joy walked back to the circulation desk to join her colleague behind the counter, I wandered over to the shelves that she had indicated. The selection was great for a small library; I took several books and periodicals back to the table where we had been sitting. There was a periodical called *Inquiring Mind* that attracted my attention, with an article by Tara Brach called "Awakening from the Trance of Unworthiness." I took out my notebook and started taking notes.

The article began with a quote by Rainer Maria Rilke:

It's here in all the pieces of my shame
That now I find myself again.
I yearn to belong to something, to be contained
In an all-embracing mind that sees me . . .

That line, "all the pieces of my shame," struck me. I had been immersed in shame for so long. The discounting of compliments, doubting people's sincerity, the overwhelming feeling inside that something was sorely lacking—not only that I didn't have enough but that *I* simply was not enough. I copied the poem into my notebook and reread it several times, letting it sink in, feeling it in my bones, that yearning to belong.

I took a deep breath and began to take notes from Brach's article: "Our most fundamental sense of well-being is derived from the conscious experience of belonging. When we feel part of the whole, connected to our bodies, to each other, and the living Earth, there is a sense of inherent rightness, of being wakeful and in love. The experience of universal belonging is at the heart of all mystical traditions."

I smiled as I remembered the conversation in Sun Valley about Unity. And I remembered the conversations in Boulder, and the quote by Johann Hari that Rachel had shared: "The opposite of addiction isn't sobriety. It's connection." I had the surreal feeling that all of my life's lessons were aligning. As I continued reading the article, I wrote: "Feeling separate is an existential trance in which we have forgotten the wholeness of our being."

I got chills as I continued to read Brach's words, echoing the words I had read in the book Stacy had given me in Sun Valley by Michael Beckwith: that we believe life happens to us, then many of us begin to believe that life happens by us, giving us a false sense of control. Brach explained that this sense of control might feel empowering at first, but then causes fear and pain:

'Life happens, emotions well up, sensations arise, events come and go, and we then add on to the experiences that they are happening to me, because of me. When inevitable pain arises, we take it personally. We are diagnosed with a disease or go through a divorce, and we perceive that we are the cause of unpleasantness (we're deficient), or that we are the weak and vulnerable victims of events (still deficient). Since everything that happens reflects on me, when something seems wrong, the source of wrong is me. The defining characteristic of the trance of separation is this feeling and fearing of deficiency. Feeling "not good enough" is that often-unseen engine that drives our daily behavior and life choices. Fear of failure and rejection feeds addictive behavior. We become trapped in workaholism—an endless striving to accomplish—and we overconsume to numb the persistent presence of fear.'

I was furiously writing. Each word felt important. It all connected back to addiction again; we get trapped in trying to numb the persistent presence of fear. Once again, I recognized that alignment of everything I had been learning on this trip, the Rubik's Cube clicking into place.

Brach described hitting a boundary and defined it as the trance of unworthiness:

'I had a tendency to believe something was wrong with me. Wrong if I was fatigued, wrong if my mind was wandering, wrong if I was anxious, wrong if I was depressed. The overlay of shame converted unpleasant experiences into a verdict on self. Pain turned into suffering. In the moment that I made myself wrong, the world got small and tight . . . I was in the trance of unworthiness.'

*The trance of unworthiness*, that concept encapsulated what I had felt for so long. I took a deep breath and closed my eyes. I had let that trance rule my life. I had believed that I didn't deserve love or fulfillment; I had searched for a remedy to that deeply painful wound in substances and behaviors that only served to make me feel worse about myself. That experience of shame, as feeling fundamentally deficient, was so excruciating that I did whatever I could to avoid it. Most addicts I knew, hell, most people I knew, would do almost anything to numb themselves from these feelings: staying physically busy and mentally preoccupied; overeating, overdrinking, overusing any substances available. And then once clean and sober, most people I knew in recovery would jump into endless self-improvement projects. It seemed like a never-ending cycle.

Brach described a need for a paradigm shift:

'Rather than hiding in addictive behaviors or climbing up a ladder, seeking perfection, we are unfolding into wholeness. We are not trying to transcend or vanquish the difficult energies that we consider wrong—the fear, shame, jealousy, anger. This only creates a shadow that fuels our sense of deficiency. Rather, we are learning to turn around and embrace life in all its realness—broken, messy, vivid, alive.'

That's it! Embrace all of our messy and vivid life, even be grateful for it, as Joy had been describing. But how do we do that?

I saw a quote by Danna Faulds in the magazine: "All you ever longed for is before you in this moment, if you dare draw in a breath and whisper 'Yes.'"

There it was, all the secrets coming together again. *Life's Secrets* had been incredibly important to learn, and I realized that in addition to these secrets, true healing and freedom would only become possible if I included the shadow, all of those unwanted parts of myself in full compassionate awareness. As part of my Fusion Recovery, I realized that I would have to work with that *trance of unworthiness*—that I would have to stop running from everything that I thought was wrong with myself, practice what Brach called the *sacred art of pausing*; stop the fear-driven busyness, and learn to pause frequently, breathe, and just be.

I looked up at the clock and realized that I had been in the library for several hours. I needed some food and some sunshine. I looked over and saw that there was a lull at the circulation desk, so I wrote down the names of the books that I hadn't had a chance to look at and put the pile on the reshelve cart nearby, then went up to Joy at the desk. "Thank you again for your time and energy," I told her. "This has been amazing. I feel like so much has fallen into place."

"I wrote down a few names and online talks and podcasts that I thought you might enjoy. And I wrote down a quote by a wonderful professor of psychology and psychiatry named Dr. Richard Davidson. I was fortunate to hear him speak last year in Boston." Joy read the words aloud: "'We need a different conception of happiness, more enduring and more genuine, not dependent on external circumstances. Happiness and well-being are actually best regarded as skills, something that can be cultivated. Everything we've learned about the brain suggests it's no different than learning the violin . . . if you practice, you'll get better at it.'" She came around the desk to give me a hug. "So keep practicing, dear Meg, stay steadfast on your journey."

I had tears in my eyes as I hugged Joy tight. "Thank you, Joy. Thank you so much, I am incredibly grateful for all you've shared with me today. And I shall focus on you and your kindness for much more than that recommended fifteen seconds."

———

I walked home slowly in the late afternoon sunshine. I took time to watch the squirrels playing in the trees and to listen to the birdsong. The walk in town was alive with activity, colors, and sounds that I usually would not have noticed. I met people's eyes and smiled and was pleased with the number of people who smiled back.

When I finally got home that evening, I sent a long audio to my sons, expressing my deep gratitude for who they are as people and for the relationship we had built as a family. I made myself a cup of tea and sat down to write in my journal.

*Day Twenty—Northampton, MA*

*This is it, my last night. Tomorrow I arrive in Boston, the end of my journey.*

*Today has been a gift beyond measure. What a fantastic stroke of luck to meet Joy the librarian, what a beautiful soul. And reading about the trance of unworthiness, wow, that reached deep into my core, reminding me again to say yes to all of my imperfect and messy life, to accept me as I am, warts and all.*

*All of the pieces are fitting together, everything I've been learning through my Life's Lessons are aligning.*

*And now, twenty-one days later, at the end of my journey, so many people, so many places . . . I want to thank that woman I met in the dream, the one that sparked the idea for this trip, to discover for myself the secrets to life. I am grateful beyond measure to her, and so grateful that I paid attention.*

*Secret #8*

*Gratitude is absolutely the next secret.*

*Gratitude and escaping the trance of unworthiness . . .*
*Embracing all of me, shadow side, deficits, and all.*

BOSTON, MA

## CHAPTER 13

*"We're all just walking each other home."*
—RAM DASS

I woke up feeling languid, twisting my body slowly, feeling warm
and relaxed, breathing evenly. I realized that in the past, I had often
woken up feeling anxious, like I had awakened from a bad dream
that I couldn't remember, but still felt a sense of dread. But this
morning I felt hopeful; I felt at home in my skin.

I got up and made a cup of tea and got back into bed. I was in no
hurry to jump up and get moving. The drive to Boston was only about
two hours, and I wanted to take my time and just enjoy my morning.
I wrote a few pages in the journal, exploring this new hopeful feeling,
and wrote a few things I felt grateful for at that moment, then did a
short meditation and set an intention for the day. I knew it would
require some self-discipline to stay the course with my Fusion Recovery plan but felt committed to the path.

I checked the time and realized it was too early to call Nella, but
since Rosie was such a night owl, she might still be awake. I messaged
her to find out if she was awake, and a few seconds later, the phone
rang.

"Hey, Meg, I was just thinking about you," she said warmly. "I'm sitting outside on the porch, sipping my tea, wrapped up in a blanket, enjoying the clear sky and brilliant stars. I was just about to finish my tea and head to bed when I got your message. Perfect timing. Where are you? What's happening?"

"Oh, it's so wonderful to hear your voice," I said, delighted that she had answered. "I'm just lying in bed about to start my day but wanted to touch base with you, my dear friend. I'm in Northampton, about to start the last day of my journey. Hopefully by the end of today, I will be dipping my toes in the Atlantic Ocean and will have done it, driven coast-to-coast."

"Well done, sister! How are you feeling?"

"Oh, Rosie, I am feeling so good. It's odd, well, maybe odd isn't the right word, different from how I usually feel anyway . . . I feel so at peace . . . and so . . . hopeful is the word I came up with."

"'Hope is the thing with feathers that perches in the soul—and sings the tune without the words—and never stops at all.' My very favorite quote by Emily Dickenson. Hope can be so elusive; when it comes to visit, it feels like such a lovely gift."

"Oh, I need to write that down. I love it. I am going to put that up in my room when I get home."

What a perfect quote. I stood up, put my bag on the bed, and got my notebook and pen out, while Rosie waited patiently.

"This is the second quote in two days that has really moved me. Yesterday I met a wonderful librarian in Northampton who shared a quote about gratitude and eventually helped me put a few more pieces together in my puzzle. I'm feeling more hopeful than I have in so many years; it's just kind of miraculous."

"Oh, honey, I'm so happy for you, this all sounds just amazing. What a journey."

I walked over to the window and looked out at the day. I felt a real sense of accomplishment knowing that I was on my last day of the trip.

"I can't wait to share it all face to face with you, Rosie. I feel like I'm ready to come home, ready to start a new chapter, ready to start that Fusion Recovery meeting with you."

"Yes! I am so looking forward to all of that. We have big plans, my friend."

"But for now, I better head out soon. I decided to splurge for my last night; I booked a room at Nantasket Beach Resort. It's outside my budget, but what the hell, it's a celebration. The beach looks like a great place to put my feet in the water and celebrate the end of the journey."

The day was beckoning to me to get on the road; I started pulling my things together to get out.

"You go for it, girl! OK, enjoy your last leg, have fun, and have a splash in the Atlantic for me. Call me whenever you can, OK?"

"OK, will do, Rosie, my friend. I love you."

"I love you too. Big hugs."


The drive that day was easy, and as I was arriving at Nantasket Beach, I played the last song on the playlist, "Boston" by Augustana. As I listened to the song, tears rolled down my cheeks . . . I made it; I was here.

After I parked, I sent Nella an audio message: "I'm listening to the last song on your wonderful playlist. I'm here Nells. I'm in Boston; I made it. Your perfect playlist and beautiful fig accompanied me the whole journey. Thank you so much, my friend. I love you."

I got out of the car and stretched as I looked up at the hotel building. I was reminded of something out of a Cary Grant movie; it evoked the charm and grace of yesteryear. The oceanfront stone hotel with its floor-to-ceiling windows looking out at the Atlantic Ocean and distant lighthouses dominated the entry to the Nantasket Peninsula.

I walked into the lobby, and my eyes swept the room: the quality of light, the views, the sweeping staircase, the high ceilings and spaciousness. As I walked up to the desk, a young man smiled at me.

"Hi, I'm Nate, welcome to Nantasket Beach Resort. Do you have a reservation?" His smile lit up his face. His curly brown hair framed his face in a way that reminded me of my sons. His looks and warm demeanor reinforced how much I missed my own sons.

"Hi. Yes, I do. I'm Meg, here's my license."

"Ah, yes, your room is ready for you."

While Nate did the check-in thing, I wandered over to a board that explained what was on in the area. There was a brightly colored flyer advertising the creative arts fair. The flyer explained that the fair was along the promenade. When we finished the check-in process, I asked Nate about the arts fair.

"Oh, it's right out there, just walk out the door and walk up that way toward Hull. There are lots of booths and exhibitions from local artists. My mom has one of the booths, actually. You should tell her I sent you."

I smiled and was reminded of my own sons. "I'll do that. What's her name and where can I find her?"

"Her name is Juliette. She has a booth supporting the creative arts in the region. I helped her set up yesterday; she's in a blue gazebo thing about halfway down, with a big sign that says, 'Support the Arts.' You can't miss it. She teaches art over at the community college in Quincy. She's a great artist and a really good teacher," he said. I hoped my sons spoke about me in the same way that this young man did about his mom.

"Well, Nate, I will absolutely look for her and tell her that she has a lovely son." He smiled shyly and I headed upstairs.

I opened the door of my room with glee, alternating between feeling very grown up alone in this gorgeous establishment and at the same time wanting to go jump on the bed with exuberance. My eye first went to the sparkling ocean view just beyond the balcony, and then I circled back to the luxurious king-sized bed with the brilliant white puffy comforter and large pillows. The room smelled clean with a faint hint of lemon. Yes, it was a splurge, but what a fabulous way to end the journey.

"I deserve this. This is ultimate self-care," I said out loud on the balcony. Part of me wanted to just hang out here, but for now, I would get down to the water to conclude my coast-to-coast expedition. I changed clothes, put on my sunglasses, and headed down to the beach.

When I stepped into the chilly Atlantic surf, I closed my eyes, lifted my face to the sun, and threw out my arms. "I'm here. I made it. Well done, Meg, you did it," I said aloud. After a few minutes with my eyes shut and my face lifted, as the surf lapped up around my ankles and calves, the noise from the families on the beach faded away, and I felt like I was the only person on the planet, just me and the ocean. I felt like I was floating in the ocean, rather than simply standing on the shore. Sparkles of light flashed behind my closed eyelids and my ears started buzzing. It was a similar feeling to the one I had had during Tara Brach's meditation—that feeling that my body was expanding—my head and hands started inflating like I might float away. Again, I wasn't frightened. It felt spiritual and expansive . . . I felt like I was connected to all living things.

The moment passed, but I felt somehow cleansed by it, sharper, clearer, and definitely lighter. I opened my eyes slowly and came back to the present moment. I stepped back from the water and dropped down wobbly to the warm sand, slightly dizzy. I wasn't sure what the experience meant, but my body was buzzing, I felt electrified amid my connection to myself, to others, and to the earth.

When I felt like my legs could carry me again, I got up and walked back up to the promenade and took my time, appreciating the artwork and interesting crafts on display. I saw the blue gazebo up ahead, just as Nate had promised. As I approached the stall, I saw a sign tacked up behind the table: "'Creativity can solve almost any problem. The creative act, the defeat of habit by originality, overcomes everything.'— George Lois"

Another quote—they seemed to be popping up everywhere. I wondered if these profound statements had been around me before and I hadn't noticed, or if my shifting consciousness was now attracting them to me somehow.

Behind the table, at the stall, stood a tall, willowy woman, about my own age. She was putting on a jacket and talking to another woman at the stall. I was sure it was Juliette.

As she was leaving the stall, I approached her. "You must be Juliette," I said with a smile of recognition; Nate inherited his eyes from his mother.

She smiled. "You're right. Are you here to support the arts in our area? We're gathering signatures to stop the cutting of funds to our arts programs in schools."

I smiled as I took the pen and clipboard and signed my name. On the top of the petition, it said: "Creativity deserves a seat at the table."

Juliette took the clipboard back and said: "The local government here is trying to save money, and so of course the first thing they want to do is take money away from anything that involves creativity in the curriculum. That's why we have coined our cause 'Creativity deserves a seat at the table.' We are fighting to keep the arts in the curriculum."

"Nate told me you were passionate about art and teaching."

She beamed. "Oh, do you know my son? What a wonderful surprise. You know I'm Juliette, what is your name?" she said as she held out her hand.

"Hi, Juliette, I'm Meg. I only just met him today at the hotel, but he's obviously very proud of you. I hope my sons speak as highly of me as Nate does about you."

"Oh, he is a gem, my Nate. I'm a single mother, and I've raised two boys on a teacher's salary, which is not an easy feat, I assure you."

"Me too. I mean, I'm on my own as well, raising two sons, although they are more young men than boys now."

"Ha. Yeah, mine too. But they'll always be my boys."

I nodded in agreement. "Well, Nate is a very special young man; you've obviously done a wonderful job."

Juliette smiled, but her upturned mouth didn't quite reach her eyes. I wondered what was behind the look. I was drawn to hug her or comfort her somehow but didn't say anything, having just met the woman.

"I was going to the coffee truck over there to grab a latté. I've been here since seven, and I need a break," she said. "Would you like to join me?"

I was touched by the invitation. "That would be really nice, thank you."

We walked together to the truck, bought our coffees, and then sat on a bench near the beach.

"Thank you for saying that about Nate. It's really lovely to hear," Juliette said quietly. "It's not been an easy journey since Nate's dad died about seven years ago."

"Oh, God." My heart bled for her. "I can only imagine how hard that must be."

Juliette sighed and shrugged and then changed the subject. "How about you? What brings you to Nantasket?"

"Well, it's kind of a long story, but I'll try to condense," I said with a chuckle. "I live in New Zealand now but am from California. My dad died, and I came back to bury him and take care of all the stuff that comes after death. And I just felt like I needed some time to sort some things out, so I decided to travel coast-to-coast to take some time for myself. I'm in recovery, so I'm calling it my recovery road trip." I raised my eyebrows, "And here I am on the other coast."

Juliette smiled. "That is a great story. Sorry about your dad, though."

"Oh, it's OK, we've been estranged for years," I said matter-of-factly. "It's never fun dealing with all that stuff, but I got through it. And this road trip has been a godsend; I've met some incredible people."

"You mentioned you're in recovery?" she prompted.

I nodded.

"Good for you. My husband died of an overdose." Juliette paused and looked out at the ocean. I waited quietly until she continued. "I've been attending Al-Anon for years. It saved me, it really did. It still breaks my heart that David, Nate's dad, died in such a horrible way, but the real heartbreak at the moment is dealing with Nate's older brother, Chris. He's using now and living on the street in Boston." Tears ran down Juliette's face as she looked out to sea; she pulled a tissue out of her pocket and blew her nose. "Ugh. Please forgive me. I don't even know you and I'm pouring all of this on you."

"Oh, please don't apologize," I said. "I'm so honored that you're sharing this with me. As an addict myself, I really feel your pain."

"Most of my friends are in Al-Anon or some form of recovery," she said. "Nate's brother has been in and out of treatment. I keep praying that recovery will get its hooks in him, deeper than the fentanyl has, but that hasn't happened yet. My husband got in a bad car accident and was prescribed oxycodone as a pain reliever; that's what started it all. After a while, Chris started taking some of David's pills occasionally, then he hurt himself rather badly skateboarding, and he got his own supply. It makes me sick that I didn't know enough then to stop him. I wish I could turn back time and go back with the knowledge I have today." Juliette took a deep breath and watched the waves breaking for a couple of minutes. "After my husband died, I tried to control Chris to get him to stop, until eventually I went to Al-Anon. I was so distraught trying to get Chris to stop that I was ignoring Nate when he needed me most. Thank goodness I didn't lose him too. I think after seeing Chris's deterioration, he decided to steer clear of drugs, thank God. Now Chris comes home when he gets too desperate; I feed him, put him to bed, buy him new clothes, and pray he'll stay home; but so far he's continued to go back on the streets." Juliette dabbed her eyes and blew her nose. She sighed and continued, "Chris was the one who found his dad, dead in the bathroom; he was only eighteen."

"Oh my God, I'm so sorry, how traumatic."

"Indeed. I've read a lot about trauma and addiction since then. There is one doctor, Dr. Gabor Maté, have you heard of him?"

"Yes!" I told Juliette about Rachel in Boulder; inside I felt the now familiar electric current up my spine: the Life's Lessons overlapping again.

Juliette continued, "I love the way he describes trauma, that it's not what happens to you, it's what happens inside you. Well, finding his father dead broke something inside Chris. He just disconnected, from his emotions and from his body. Dr. Maté says that addiction is not the primary problem, that addiction is the attempt to solve the problem. Chris's pain was too much . . . He wanted to numb it away, and fentanyl did a great job at that. In the therapy we did together in his first stint in rehab, we learned that if Chris could reconnect with himself, by restoring the connection with his body and his emotions, then there would be room for recovery. Because as they explained to us, recovery is recovering something, finding it again, and what happens in recovery is that we can find ourselves again. They explained that that loss of self is the essence of trauma, that the path to recovery starts with restoring that connection to that self that was lost in the trauma."

We stared out at the water for a few minutes, sipping our coffee in silence. The moment felt sacred, and I didn't want to destroy it with the wrong words.

Juliette was the one to finally take a deep breath and speak again: "That's one of the reasons that I'm so passionate about creativity and keeping creativity in the curriculum, available to everyone. It's been a lifeline for me. And it's been proven time and again, study after study, that creativity reduces anxiety, depression, and stress, and it can also help to process trauma. In short, creativity reconnects you to yourself."

"Were you always an artist and art teacher?" I asked as I finished my coffee.

"Well, I've always loved to paint and sketch, but I thought of it as my little hobby," she said with a little smile. "But when David died, I wanted to do work that would make a difference, so I went back to school, studied art and creativity, and got my teaching certificate. I loved doing research about creativity. The link between the unconscious and practicing any form of creativity is a fascinating one. There are a lot of studies showing how doing anything creative can be therapeutic for people suffering from depression, anxiety, and PTSD. When I'm teaching art, I always emphasize that there is no right way to do art. I'm not teaching technique, but instead hopefully holding a space where creativity can happen. And hopefully this space will give participants in the class an outlet for expressing and releasing their feelings and fears. To be perfectly honest, I don't care what my students create; I just hope they find a way to express their creativity. What I attempt to do with every class is to allow a process of creation where my students take themselves down a path of self-discovery; I hope it helps them eliminate their own emotional roadblocks. I guess I feel that if I can't help my son heal and reconnect with himself, then maybe I can help someone else do some healing."

"Wow. Man, I wish you were teaching near me." I shook my head. "I'd love to join one of your classes."

Juliette smiled, "Thank you, Meg, that is kind. I'm sure there are some excellent teachers near you; you should look into taking some classes once you get home." Juliette took out her phone to check the clock. "Oh my goodness, look at the time, I better get back to the stall. Thank you so much for listening, Meg, you have made my day."

"Oh, thank you, Juliette, for your honesty and your vulnerability. I'm so grateful to Nate for directing me to you. Good luck with your petition and your classes. You're a remarkable woman."

We hugged goodbye and parted ways.

Fifteen minutes later, sitting in the sand back at the beach, sipping a smoothie, I thought back to the beginning of the trip, viscerally remembering the feeling of desperation as I embarked on this journey. I hadn't been sure then exactly what I was looking for, but now I felt like I had somehow found it. I marveled at the grace that had somehow led me to each person that I needed to learn something from. I silently thanked the Universe for quietly guiding me on the journey. I thought of Joy back at Forbes Library in Northampton as I looked out at the ocean; I said thank you and paused for fifteen seconds to let my overwhelming gratitude in that moment really sink in.

After enjoying my view of the ocean a while longer, I meandered back to the hotel to go for a swim and enjoy the amenities that afternoon. On my way there, I passed a parked car with a bumper sticker saying: We're All Just Walking Each Other Home.

I stopped and stared at the bumper sticker for minute, feeling the chills race up and down my spine, then I pulled out my phone and texted my sons: "I'm coming home."


Later, on my balcony, I left an audio for Rosie:

"Hi, Rosie. I'm here; I made it. I have soaked my feet in the Atlantic Ocean. I can't wait to share everything with you when I get home. I'll be home soon, and we will start our Fusion Recovery meeting; we'll welcome people no matter what their addiction, where we share our vital connection. Oh, Rosie, I'm so excited to come home. I love you, my friend, thanks for sharing this journey with me."

I sat and watched the sky grow darker and the ocean go from a dark turquoise to deep navy blue. I could hear the waves rolling up on the sand and then receding into the sea. My shoulders were soft, and my hips sank into the cushion on the chair. I took a breath and pulled out my journal for the last time.

*Day Twenty-One—Boston, MA*

*What an amazing day today, this last day of my recovery road trip.*

*Today I learned about creativity and how it can help with trauma and addiction. I felt it deep in my bones when Juliette was talking to me, that creativity is an important piece in my recovery, that is a key element in healing that gaping hole that I tried to fill with substances and busyness. I can tell that it will be an important ingredient to add to my Fusion Recovery. I read a slogan today: "Creativity deserves a seat at the table." And it deserves a place in my recovery.*

*I had another amazing experience in the ocean today. It's so hard to get my head around it, and I don't know if I can find the words . . .*

*As I was standing in the surf, everything faded away; it was just me and the ocean, like I was floating away or, more accurately, becoming part of the ocean . . . spiritual and expansive, like I was connected to every living thing . . . a feeling of true unity.*

*And speaking of unity, I want to look back through my journal now to recount the Life Secrets that I have learned from people I've met on this journey.*

*Love—from both Nella and Rosie way back in Seattle and Missoula*

*Unity—from Stacy and Melody in Sun Valley*

*Compassion—from Kristen Neff at the Grand Canyon*

*Kindness—from Saskia in Taos*

*Yes—from a speaker at a meeting in Lincoln, Nebraska*

*Forgiveness—from my beautiful sponsor Tina in Madison*

*Intention—from a yoga instructor and Tara Brach at Kripalu Center*

*Gratitude—from Joy, the librarian in Northampton*

I read the entry again, shook my head, and reread it. Then I dropped my journal. "Oh my God!" I jumped up, ran inside, fell back on the bed, and sank deeply into the duvet. I grabbed my phone and called Nella.

My heart was beating in my throat as Nella picked up her phone.

"Meg, I was just thinking of you. I was hoping it was you ringing."

"Oh my God, Nells, I am shaking. I have to tell you something."

"Oh no, Meg, are you OK? Are you alright? Are you hurt?"

I shook my head vigorously as though Nella and I were sitting together sharing this moment in person. "No, no, nothing like that, Nell, I just made the most amazing discovery."

"Tell me!"

"Well, I was just journaling now, kind of significant, my last entry on the trip. And I was writing down all the Life's Secrets I've learned, and you won't believe what I found."

"What? Tell me." I could hear the urgency in her voice.

"Go get a pen and paper, I'll wait." I could almost see the impatient eye-rolling on her part. I heard her sigh and scratch around for a pen and paper.

"OK, OK, I'm back," she said impatiently.

"I want you to write each of these secrets in a column, one under the other, OK?"

"Mmmm, yeah go ahead." I could hear her trying to figure out what was going on.

"Love, Unity, Compassion, Kindness, Yes, Forgiveness, Intention, Gratitude. Have you got them all written in a column?"

"Yeeesss?" I could hear Nella's confusion.

"OK, put the first letter of each word next to each other . . . What does it say?"

There was a long pause; I could hear Nella's breath as she was working out the puzzle.

"Um, let me see, uh . . . L-U-C-K-Y-F-I-G. Lucky fig . . . Oh my God! Holy shit!"

I clapped my hands, tingling sensations running up and down my body. "I know, Nells, your beautiful fig; she was my guide! I have chills."

"I have chills too. Holy shit. That is so intense. Meg, when I made the fig, I took it out of the kiln, and I had this deep-body knowing that it was for you. I almost dropped it because it was like I heard a voice in my head telling me to give it to you. I didn't say anything to you because it felt insane."

We were both quiet for a while as the information settled around us. We both listened to each other breathe on the other end of the phone, letting it all sink in.

"Oh, Nells, I know, anyone listening to us would think we were crazy. But I know that beautiful lucky fig was my guide on this journey. I was led to exactly the person I was supposed to meet and what I was supposed to learn. I cannot express to you how grateful I am. Thank you so much."

Nella was quiet for a minute and then whispered, "I feel a bit like a witch . . . and I like it a lot."

"Oh, Nells, I've always known you were a witch, and I love it."

We sat quietly on the phone, not needing to say a word, just being together. I closed my eyes, my body sinking deeper into the feather duvet on the bed, feeling like I was floating on a cloud.

"Are you coming back here soon, Meg?"

"I leave tomorrow, driving straight through. I'm hoping to be back in Seattle in a few days. I'll call you from the road."

"Will you stay here for a while when you get back?"

"No, I don't think so, Nells. Thanks for offering, but I'm finally ready to go home."

I sat back against the headboard, listening to the surf. The moon was out and reflecting on the water. And, slowly, one of the beacons from a lighthouse shined right into the room as it guided boats safely to shore.

# PART TWO

## Recovery Road Trip: The Workbook

---

## WEEKLY EXERCISES

*"I want to write, but more than that, I want to bring out all kinds of things that lie buried in my heart."*
—ANNE FRANK

# Introduction

As I said at the beginning of the book, this book is an allegorical narrative, but it is born out of my own experience. One of the things that has been invaluable in my recovery and in my life in general has been journaling and the writing process. I first used this as a tool for my healing before I was ever in recovery. Then once I got sober the first time, in 1988, I wrote daily, prolifically for several years, and it was instrumental in my healing. I find writing so helpful with that feeling of frustration and grief when I feel stuck. So in writing this book and this workbook, I am hopeful that it will help other women in their own healing. And that hopefully encourages some women to explore writing as a creative modality leading to healing.

It is my hope that Meg's story has inspired you in some way on your path to healing. I invite you to undertake your own transformative journey in the workbook that follows. The workbook spans twelve weeks. It requires prioritizing yourself and making a time commitment to yourself that you hold sacred.

Morning pages are a great way to start the day and to focus. However, each day you will be assigned tasks for the day, and it is helpful to journal about your experience once you have performed the task. So I suggest you read the task for the day first thing in the morning, and then journal before bed, looking back on the day. However, if you are able to journal first thing in the morning as well, that's an excellent time to get your creative juices flowing. But what is most important is that you are uninterrupted and that you give your-self the time and space to explore.

What you will need:

- A journal

- A commitment to yourself for at least the next twelve weeks

- At least fifteen minutes each day, uninterrupted, to write (preferably longer if you are able)

When you start on this adventure of journaling and exploration, I hope you are able to buy yourself a journal that you love. Enjoy how it looks and smells and feels in your hands. Treat yourself to a journal that you get excited about. You can decide if you want the journal to be lined, to guide your writing, or if you want blank pages so you can draw and get creative within the pages. Either one is fine; just decide which one you are most comfortable with.

Each week introduces a specific area of focus, accompanied by daily topics and ideas for journaling, but please feel free to extrapolate. The process roughly follows Meg's journey by exploring the secrets to life that she learned: Love, Unity, Compassion, Kindness, Yes, Forgiveness, Intention, and Gratitude. And of course, Creativity deserves a seat at that table too.

Each week will include at least one visualization or meditation. I have recorded all of these, and you can find them all on my YouTube page:

https://www.youtube.com/user/PattiKClark

I invite you to do these meditations as often as you can. I have found them so important in my healing process.

Some of you may find the process freeing and fun; others may find that it brings up painful memories and even past trauma. If this is the case, please contact a professional. There are many wonderful therapists out there, and they can be a tremendous help in this healing journey.

I hope you enjoy this process of exploring your potential and learning to live with greater passion and purpose in *Recovery Road Trip: The Workbook.*

# Creating a Journaling Routine and Exploring Expressive Writing

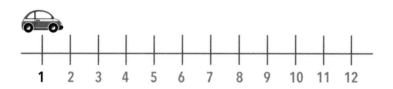

1  2  3  4  5  6  7  8  9  10  11  12

*"It always seems impossible until it's done."*

—NELSON MANDELA

## DAY ONE – JUST START WRITING

Congratulations! Taking the first step in any journey is always the hardest. This week the focus is on journaling and exploring motivation and developing a routine where you prioritize yourself. Perhaps you have been journaling for years, or maybe this is your first time. It takes time to develop a routine of writing daily.

The website for American Addiction Centers states: "Journaling is an effective tool for anyone who is recovering from an addiction. Some claim that it is the cheapest and most easily available form of therapy. It not only helps to reduce stress and improves mental health, but it may even lower the risk of relapse. Journaling is also a way to track progress and increase motivation. The benefits of keeping a journal are undeniable."

So with that in mind, let's start today! Write it all out. Just begin free-flow about yourself. Explore your personal journey.

---

- Write about why you are embarking on this journey. Be curious! Ask yourself questions about the journey and about yourself.

- Write about where you are in your life at this point in time.

- Why did you read the book in the first place? How did the book make you feel?

- Take a moment and close your eyes—ask yourself what you want to get out of the next twelve weeks. Listen to that "small, still voice"—journal about what comes up.

*"The journey of self-awareness does not create a particularly pretty form of writing. It is not often flowery, or even flattering, but it is an extremely effective form of inner communication."*

—CHRISTINA BALDWIN,
author of *Life's Companion: Journal Writing as Spiritual Practice*

## DAY TWO – DESCRIBE YOUR JOURNEY SO FAR

Today's focus will be exploring your own life's journey.

---

- Describe your life's journey so far. This can be as a story, as prose, or even just as a chronological list—whatever feels easy and flowing for you. This should not feel laborious.

- Are you where you had imagined you would be in your life now?

- Are you proud of yourself? Why?

- Are you disappointed in yourself? Why?

*"Visualization is daydreaming with a purpose."*
—BO BENNETT

## DAY THREE – CREATIVE VISUALIZATION

The purpose of today's visualization is to set up your Creative Space.

This first visualization is very simple. It is a basic introduction to the process. Imagine a special space that you create within your mind. Make it your own sacred space that you will return to, hopefully often. When you are finished, acknowledge the process in whatever way feels comfortable for you. Perhaps use Shakti Gawain's words from her book *Creative Visualization*:

This or something better,
now manifests for me
in totally satisfying and harmonious ways,
for the highest good of all concerned.

The complete visualization can be found on my YouTube page: Go to https://www.youtube.com/user/PattiKClark

---

Now Journal:

- Write it all out. Just begin free-flow to describe your experience.

- What did you see? What did you feel? What was your experience?

- Just allow the free-flow writing to express the experience of the visualization.

*"Only I can change my life. No one can do it for me."*

—CAROL BURNETT

## DAY FOUR – EXPRESSIVE WRITING

Today we are going to explore the concept of "Expressive Writing."

James Pennebaker explores this concept in *The Association of Psychological Science*. In his landmark research project, Pennebaker developed an expressive writing prompt to uncover the potential health benefits of writing about emotional upheaval.

Expressive writing comes from innermost thoughts and feelings; it's what I mean when I say just write free-form. It is personal and emotional writing without paying attention to any writing conventions, like spelling, punctuation, and verb agreement; it simply expresses what is on your mind and in your heart. This writing is for your eyes only.

- Remember, expressive writing comes from innermost thoughts and feelings, just let it flow.

- Write for a minimum of fifteen minutes.

- Write continuously: do not worry about punctuation, spelling, and grammar. If you run out of things to say, write that—that you don't know what to say—but don't stop writing. Keep pen on paper.

- Choose one prompt and write about it at length or write a bit about each prompt.

Prompt:

- Describe your writing self. Who is the *you* that is writing? How do you experience the *you* that is writing? Stand back and be the observer and describe this "journaling being" that is you.

- "Describing myself—these adjectives come to mind."

- I struggle most with . . . I am most at ease when I . . .

## DAY FIVE – WRITING TO HEAL

The American Psychological Association explains that writing strengthens people's immune systems as well as their minds: "Writing about emotions and stress can boost immune functioning in people." University of Rochester Medical Center describes the many ways that journaling helps in healing and in improving overall mental health.

Journaling can help you:

- Manage anxiety
- Reduce stress
- Cope with depression

Journaling helps control your symptoms and improve your mood by:

- Helping you prioritize problems, fears, and concerns
- Tracking any symptoms day-to-day so that you can recognize triggers and learn ways to better control them
- Providing an opportunity for positive self-talk and identifying negative thoughts and behaviors

When you have a problem and you're stressed, keeping a journal can help you identify what's causing that stress or anxiety.

Today, look at some stressors in your life.

Use the expressive writing technique explained yesterday to explore what is causing you stress or anxiety. Don't worry about how to solve the problems, just take time to explore them.

Write a letter to yourself; write as though writing to your best friend. Express that you are there for her and that you will support her through any challenges.

*"Quality is not an act, it is a habit."*
—ARISTOTLE

## DAY SIX – DEVELOPING A JOURNALING HABIT

Watch your thoughts; they become words.
Watch your words; they become actions.
Watch your actions; they become habits.
Watch your habits; they become character.
Watch your character; for it becomes your destiny."
—UPANISHADS

Even if you're not a person who usually thrives by having a routine, it can be very useful, especially for developing new habits.

- The first thing to do to develop a habit is to make it habitual. Obvious, I know, but it is often the hardest hurdle to overcome.

- Set the same time every day, a time that feels spacious and not hurried. The actual time doesn't matter, as long as it works for you.

- If you're a morning person, wake up fifteen to twenty minutes earlier and write morning pages, just write free-flow. This is also a great time to write down your dreams from the previous night if you remember them.

- If afternoons and evenings feel more spacious, then make it an evening activity, but make sure you do it before you get too tired at the end of the day.

- Just make sure it becomes something you schedule for yourself every day. You can even set a reminder for yourself.

- Decide on the timing that works for you. Journal about the timing that you commit to and write about why you are committing to a journaling habit and why you think that this is an important habit to start for yourself.

*"When you catch a glimpse of your potential,*
*that's when passion is born."*
—ZIG ZIGLAR

## DAY SEVEN – LOOKING BACK AND MOVING FORWARD

Congratulations! You have finished the first week.

---

- Look back over the week. Write free-flow about the week and what you have noticed about developing the journaling habit and how you are feeling about the journey so far and the journey to come. Has it been easier or harder than you imagined? Why?

- Make a commitment for next week with yourself to keep up the momentum.

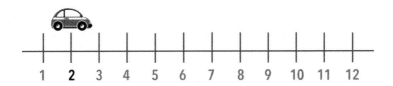

1   2   3   4   5   6   7   8   9   10   11   12

*"Self-love seems so often unrequited."*

—ANTHONY POWELL

## DAY ONE – EXPLORING SELF-LOVE

This week we will be exploring the idea of self-love.

---

- How do you treat yourself?
- Honestly, how do you talk to yourself and take care of yourself?
- Explore this topic, writing free-flow.

*"Love creates a communion with life. Love expands us, connects us, sweetens us, ennobles us. Love springs up in tender concern, it blossoms into caring action. It makes beauty out of all we touch. In any moment we can step beyond our small self and embrace each other as beloved parts of a whole."*

—JACK KORNFIELD

## DAY TWO – CREATING A SELF-LOVE ROUTINE

Today we're going to start a routine that I encourage you to continue, not only throughout this journaling journey, but for your lifetime.

---

- Write free-flow—what does a self-love routine look like for you?

- What types of things do you enjoy and feel are nurturing? Make a list. Write down everything you can think of, no editing, just write down everything that pops in your mind.

- Now make a commitment, in writing, to practice one piece of self-love every day this week. Make a list, one act of self-love for each day of the week.

*"You are the Michelangelo of your own life. The David that you are sculpting is you. And you do it with your thoughts."*

—JOE VITALE

## DAY THREE – CREATIVE VISUALIZATION

Today's visualization is about love, most specifically self-love.

Robert Morely believes that to fall in love with yourself is the first secret to happiness. So today you will go back to the Creative Space that you created last week. In that space, you will relax into the vision of self-love.

When you are finished, acknowledge the process in whatever way feels comfortable for you. Perhaps use Shakti Gawain's words from her book *Creative Visualization*:

> This or something better,
> now manifests for me
> in totally satisfying and harmonious ways,
> for the highest good of all concerned.

The complete visualization can be found on my YouTube page: go to https://www.youtube.com/user/PattiKClark

---

Now Journal:

- Write it all out. Just begin free-flow to describe your experience.

- What did you see? What did you feel? What was your experience?

- Just allow the free-flow writing to express the experience of the visualization.

*If you aren't good at loving yourself, you will have a difficult time loving anyone, since you'll resent the time and energy you give another person that you aren't even giving to yourself."*
—BARBARA DE ANGELIS

## DAY FOUR – EXPRESSIVE WRITING

- Remember, expressive writing comes from innermost thoughts and feelings, just let it flow.

- Write for a minimum of fifteen minutes.

- Write continuously: do not worry about punctuation, spelling, and grammar. If you run out of things to say, write that—that you don't know what to say—but don't stop writing. Keep pen on paper.

- Choose one prompt and write about it at length or write a bit about each prompt.5.05 in

Today's Prompt:

- I practice self-love by . . .

- My barriers to self-love are . . .

- If a friend came to me and said that they struggled with self-love, I would say . . .

*"Love yourself unconditionally, just as you love those closest to you despite their faults."*

—LES BROWN

## DAY FIVE – EXPRESSING SELF-LOVE: A LETTER TO SELF

- Write a letter to yourself—a real love letter, one that you might write to your true love.

- Describe in this letter what you appreciate about yourself, what you admire, what positive attributes you see—name them, be descriptive and elaborate fully.

*"Self-care is never a selfish act—it is simply good stewardship of the only gift I have, the gift I was put on earth to offer to others."*

—PARKER PALMER

## DAY SIX – THE TRANCE OF UNWORTHINESS

Tara Brach describes the trance of unworthiness as: "The way we tend to hold ourselves to impossible self-standards; the feeling we get when we fall short of those standards and self-expectations, and we berate ourselves mercilessly."

---

- Today explore this trance of unworthiness.

- Write free-flow where you hold yourself to unreasonable standards.

- What do you expect of yourself that you would not expect of others?

- What does your inner critic say to you when you fall short of those standards?

- Practice writing a few sentences of support to counteract the inner critic.

*"You yourself, as much as anybody in the entire universe deserve your love and affection."*

—BUDDHA

## DAY SEVEN – LOOKING BACK AND MOVING FORWARD

Well Done! You have finished the second week.

---

- How many days did you practice self-love and self-care this week? Look back at the list you made on day two and check in. How did you do?

- How did it feel? Write and really explore the feelings you had, the visceral somatic experience of caring for yourself and nurturing yourself. Where did it sit in the body? Describe it as fully as you can.

- Remember that quote from Buddha—you yourself deserve your love and affection. Close this week's journal entry with a short simple sentence about why you, yourself, deserve your love and affection.

*Unity*

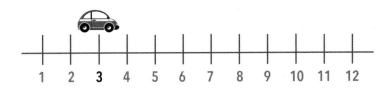

1   2   **3**   4   5   6   7   8   9   10   11   12

*"Love is the cause of unity in all things."*
—ARISTOTLE

## DAY ONE – EXPLORING THE IDEA OF UNITY

Love and unity go hand in hand. Last week we explored the concept of love, especially self-love. This week we will expand that and move into unity.

The concept of unity can be described as: the state of being undivided or unbroken, a completeness; the quality of being united into one. Unity can denote a combining of all the parts, elements, and individuals into an effective whole.

---

- How do you describe unity?
- How do you practice unity in your daily life?
- Is it important to you? Why or why not?
- If you've never really thought about it, explore that.

*"So powerful is the light of unity that it can illuminate the whole earth."*
—BAHA'U'LLAH

## DAY TWO – THE IMPORTANCE OF CONNECTION

Today we explore unity and connection. Recent studies have shown that if we want to maximize our physical health and increase our longevity, one of the most important factors to focus on is feeling connected with others, having strong social connections.

---

- How do you nurture connection in your life?

- What do you do on a daily basis to practice unity and increase connection?

- Make a commitment in writing to practice one act every day to nurture unity and connection.

*"I do believe, and I have seen in my own life,*
*that creative visualization works!"*
—OPRAH WINFREY

## DAY THREE – CREATIVE VISUALIZATION

Today's visualization is about practicing the concept of unity and connection in daily life. Brené Brown defines connection as the energy that exists between people when they feel seen, heard, and valued; when they can give and receive without judgment; and when they derive sustenance and strength from the relationship. So today you will relax into the vision of true connection.

When you are finished, acknowledge the process in whatever way feels comfortable for you. Perhaps use Shakti Gawain's words from her book *Creative Visualization*:

> This or something better,
> now manifests for me
> in totally satisfying and harmonious ways,
> for the highest good of all concerned.

The complete visualization can be found on my YouTube page: go to https://www.youtube.com/user/PattiKClark

---

Now Journal:

- Write it all out. Just begin free-flow to describe your experience.

- What did you see? What did you feel? What was your experience?

- Just allow the free-flow writing to express the experience of the visualization.

*"Life has taught us that love does not consist of gazing at each other, but in looking outward together in the same direction. There is no comradeship except through union in the same high effort."*

—ANTOINE DE SAINT-EXUPÉRY

## DAY FOUR – EXPRESSIVE WRITING

- Remember, expressive writing comes from innermost thoughts and feelings, just let it flow.

- Write for a minimum of fifteen minutes.

- Write continuously: do not worry about punctuation, spelling, and grammar. If you run out of things to say, write that—that you don't know what to say—but don't stop writing. Keep pen on paper.

- Choose one prompt and write about it at length or write a bit about each prompt.

---

Today's Prompt:

- I feel most connected to people when . . .

- My people are . . .

- Connection to people is important to me because . . .

- I can stay more connected to people by . . .

*"United we stand, divided we fall."*
—AESOP

## DAY FIVE – EXPLORING FEELINGS OF SEPARATION

- Write a letter to yourself—explore feelings of connection and separation.

- Describe in this letter when you feel most connected to yourself and others and explore when you feel most separate and isolated.

- Express to yourself that you are there for you—like you would to a good friend who is feeling lonely and alone in the world.

- Explore in this letter what you can do to feel more unity and connection with those around you.

*"He who experiences the unity of life sees his own self in all beings, and all beings in his own self, and looks on everything with an impartial eye."*

—BUDDHA

## DAY SIX – SEEING YOURSELF IN ALL BEINGS

Today, explore the idea of unity of life, seeing yourself in all beings.

---

- Have you ever had the experience of feeling unity with another person or a group of people, where you feel truly united?

- If you have, write about that; and if you haven't, write about how that might feel.

- Does the idea excite or frighten you at all? Explore the emotions you feel when you think about true unity.

*"The significance that is in unity is an eternal wonder."*
—RABINDRANATH TAGORE

**DAY SEVEN** – LOOKING BACK AND MOVING FORWARD:
FINDING WONDER IN CONNECTION

Exploring the wonder in connection and in finding our true community of like-minded people.

---

- Describe your community.

- Envision and describe the people you want in your community.

- Who are you looking for? What are their characteristics? This is a chance to explore the characteristics and qualities you seek.

- Where might you find this community? How can you find like-minded people?

- Do you feel like you have found your true community? If you have found these people, what similarities do you share?

Compassion and
the Trance of
Unworthiness

WEEK 4

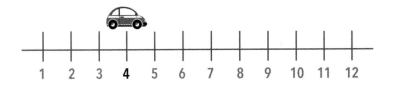

1   2   3   **4**   5   6   7   8   9   10   11   12

*"The privilege of a lifetime is being who you are."*
—JOSEPH CAMPBELL

## DAY ONE – EXPLORING SELF-COMPASSION

This week we will be exploring the idea of compassion, especially self-compassion and escaping the trance of unworthiness.

In Chapter Five, when Meg was at the Grand Canyon, she listened to a talk by Kristen Neff about self-compassion and wrote about it in her journal:

Three elements of self-compassion:

1. Self-kindness vs. Self-judgment.
2. Common humanity vs. Isolation.
3. Mindfulness vs. Over-identification.

In terms of self-kindness, Neff explained that self-compassion means being understanding toward myself when I fuck up instead of beating myself up mercilessly, that I don't have to be so self-critical and angry at myself all the time when I don't do "it" (whatever it is) right.

In terms of common humanity, I'm not the only person in the world that doesn't have it all together, that there is a shared experience, something we all go through, that it's not just me alone failing.

And self-compassion encourages me not to overfocus on me, to learn to put my own situation into a bigger perspective, learn to be more mindful and nonjudgmental, to not deny my feelings but not wallow in them either.

- Do you practice self-compassion?

- Write about the three elements of self-compassion and explore them in the context of how you treat yourself.

*"If your compassion does not include yourself, it is incomplete."*
—JACK KORNFIELD

## DAY TWO – PRACTICING SELF-COMPASSION

Today, focus on ways in which you can practice more love and compassion toward yourself. Many women find it very difficult to prioritize themselves and are unsure how to start to practice more self-compassion. Here are some ways to start:

---

- Focus on your own needs. Practice saying no to others and yes to yourself.

- Give your body the nurturing, rest, and comfort it needs.

- Accept yourself as you are, warts and all.

- Prioritize time for yourself, time to do what you love, without judgment that it is a waste of time.

- Set boundaries to protect the time you have prioritized for yourself.

- Don't keep blaming yourself for past mistakes. Learn from them and let them go.

- Go ahead and make mistakes. Everyone makes mistakes, instead of beating yourself up for it, think of it as AFOG (another fucking opportunity for growth.)

- Choose to spend time with people who put you up, not down.

- Write about any of these ideas and how you might put them into practice in your life right now.

*"To bring anything into your life, imagine that it's already there."*
—RICHARD BACH

## DAY THREE – CREATIVE VISUALIZATION

Today's visualization is about compassion, especially self-compassion.

Sandra Bierig describes self-compassion as accepting ourselves as we are, valuing our imperfections as much as our perfections. So today you will explore how it feels to be truly self-compassionate, valuing all of yourself.

When you are finished, acknowledge the process in whatever way feels comfortable for you. Perhaps use Shakti Gawain's words from her book *Creative Visualization*:

This or something better,
now manifests for me
in totally satisfying and harmonious ways,
for the highest good of all concerned.

The complete visualization can be found on my YouTube page: go to https://www.youtube.com/user/PattiKClark

---

Now Journal:

- Write it all out. Just begin free-flow to describe your experience.

- What did you see? What did you feel? What was your experience?

- Just allow the free-flow writing to express the experience of the visualization.

*"Compassion isn't some kind of self-improvement project or ideal that we're trying to live up to. Having compassion starts and ends with having compassion for all those unwanted parts of ourselves, all those imperfections that we don't even want to look at."*

—PEMA CHODRON

## DAY FOUR – EXPRESSIVE WRITING

Today, explore self-compassion through expressive writing.

By now you know the drill . . .

- Remember, expressive writing comes from innermost thoughts and feelings, just let it flow.
- Write for a minimum of fifteen minutes.
- Write continuously: do not worry about punctuation, spelling, and grammar. If you run out of things to say, write that—that you don't know what to say—but don't stop writing. Keep pen on paper.
- Choose one prompt and write about it at length or write a bit about each prompt.

---

Today's Prompt:

Self-compassion means having compassion for all those unwanted parts of ourselves, all those imperfections that we don't even want to look at.

- My worst imperfections and unwanted parts are . . .
- I'm uncomfortable with those imperfections because . . .
- Describe what practicing self-compassion would look like.

*"Talk to yourself as you would someone you love."*
—BRENÉ BROWN

## DAY FIVE – LETTER TO SELF

Write a letter to yourself.

---

- In the letter, describe how you would like to practice more compassion toward yourself.

- How do you treat a good friend if she is hurt or sad? How could you do that for yourself?

- When something goes wrong in your own life, what does your inner voice sound like? Be honest and try to transcribe what you say to yourself when something doesn't work out. If that inner voice is less than kind, try to reword it so that it sounds like what you would say to a good friend.

*"Feeling compassion for ourselves in no way releases us from responsibility for our actions. Rather, it releases us from the self-hatred that prevents us from responding to our life with clarity and balance."*

—TARA BRACH

## DAY SIX – THE TRANCE OF UNWORTHINESS

Today we are going to explore the trance of unworthiness.

In Northampton, Meg read Tara Brach's description of the trance of unworthiness: "I had a tendency to believe something was wrong with me. Wrong if I was fatigued, wrong if my mind was wandering, wrong if I was anxious, wrong if I was depressed. The overlay of shame converted unpleasant experiences into a verdict on self. Pain turned into suffering. In the moment that I made myself wrong, the world got small and tight . . . I was in the trance of unworthiness."

---

- Write about any experiences you have had in that trance of unworthiness.

- Describe that overlay of shame, about how the pain turned into suffering.

- You don't have to do anything about it, just explore how that trance has impacted your life.

*"Self-care is not selfish or self-indulgent. We cannot nurture others from a dry well. We need to take care of our own needs first, so that we can give from our surplus, our abundance. When we nurture others from a place of fullness, we feel renewed instead of taken advantage of."*

—JENNIFER LOUDEN

## DAY SEVEN – LOOKING BACK AND MOVING FORWARD: ESCAPING THE TRANCE OF UNWORTHINESS

Tara Brach explains how we can escape that trance of unworthiness: "Rather than hiding in addictive behaviors or climbing up a ladder seeking perfection, we are unfolding into wholeness. We are not trying to transcend or vanquish the difficult energies that we consider wrong—the fear, shame, jealousy, anger. This only creates a shadow that fuels our sense of deficiency. Rather, we are learning to turn around and embrace life in all its realness—broken, messy, vivid, alive."

---

- Explore how you can practice "turning around and embracing life in all its realness."

- See if you can describe one specific experience of falling into that trance of unworthiness and how you might have been able to embrace your imperfections—instead of blaming and shaming them or trying to vanquish them. This is not an easy ask, so be gentle in this exploration.

*Kindness*

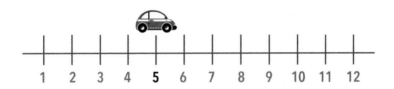

1  2  3  4  **5**  6  7  8  9  10  11  12

*"Practice random acts of kindness and senseless acts of beauty."*
—ANNE HERBERT

## DAY ONE – EXPLORING WHAT KINDNESS MEANS TO YOU

- Think about the word *kindness*. Make a list of any ideas or things that come to mind when you think of that word.

- What are some Random Acts of Kindness (RAoK) you have heard about or actually done for others or have had done for you?

- Make notes of kind things that you hear about each day, that you have seen in the community or heard about from others.

*"Carry out a random act of kindness, with no expectation of reward, safe in the knowledge that one day someone might do the same for you."*

—PRINCESS DIANA

## DAY TWO – PRACTICING RANDOM ACTS OF KINDNESS (RAoK)

Today make a list of several different Random Acts of Kindness that you will do this week. Make them varied and random! Commit to doing at least three RAoK this week.

Here are a few ideas, but feel free to add your own:

- Hold the door for the person behind you.
- Pick up litter on the beach or at a park.
- Let someone go in front of you in line.
- Give a stranger a compliment.
- Buy flowers for a friend or an acquaintance.
- Donate your old clothes to the Salvation Army.
- Help a senior with their groceries.
- Shovel a neighbor's driveway when it snows.
- Plant a tree.
- Smile at people in the street.

## DAY THREE – CREATIVE VISUALIZATION

Today's visualization is about kindness.

Jackie Chan believes that sometimes it takes only one act of kindness and caring to change a person's life. So today you will explore the concept of kindness and how kindness has the potential to change your life.

When you are finished, acknowledge the process in whatever way feels comfortable for you. Perhaps use Shakti Gawain's words from her book *Creative Visualization*:

This or something better,
now manifests for me
in totally satisfying and harmonious ways,
for the highest good of all concerned.

The complete visualization can be found on my YouTube page: go to https://www.youtube.com/user/PattiKClark

---

Now Journal:

- Write it all out. Just begin free-flow to describe your experience.

- What did you see? What did you feel? What was your experience?

- Just allow the free-flow writing to express the experience of the visualization.

*"Too often we underestimate the power of a touch, a smile, a kind word, a listening ear, an honest compliment, or the smallest act of caring, all of which have the potential to turn a life around."*

—LEO BUSCAGLIA

## DAY FOUR – EXPRESSIVE WRITING

Same exercise, new focus . . .

- Remember, expressive writing comes from innermost thoughts and feelings, just let it flow.

- Write for a minimum of fifteen minutes.

- Write continuously: do not worry about punctuation, spelling, and grammar. If you run out of things to say, write that—that you don't know what to say—but don't stop writing. Keep pen on paper.

- Choose one prompt and write about it at length or write a bit about each prompt.

---

Today's Prompt:

- Paying kindness forward can make a difference in the world by . . .

- Kindness to me means . . .

- The best way I can practice kindness toward others is by . . .

- I remember . . . (Write about an act of kindness that someone did for you and how you felt, then about an act of kindness that you did for someone else and how you felt).

*"My wish for you is that you continue. Continue to be who and how you are, to astonish a mean world with your acts of kindness. Continue to allow humor to lighten the burden of your tender heart."*

—MAYA ANGELOU

## DAY FIVE – LETTER TO SELF

Today's letter to yourself will be a conversation between yourself and your inner child. It is important for your adult self and your inner child self to talk to each other to heal. In this letter, make sure that your adult is completely kind and open, and that you have plenty of time and can work in a quiet place where you can be vulnerable. Allow yourself about an hour if possible for this exercise.

Start by writing the letter from your adult to your child. Think of speaking to yourself at about age five. Begin with: Dearest (your name) . . .

Think about what you would tell your younger self if given the chance. What would have been helpful/healing to know at that age? If you could go back in time and encourage or affirm anything to your five-year-old self, what would you say?

Take your time, take deep breaths, breathe slowly, notice any memories that may come up. Address those memories if they come up. When this feels complete, get ready to respond from your inner child.

The best way to access the voice of your inner child is to write with your nondominant hand and use a fat marker or crayon if possible. It might be helpful to use a blank piece of paper if you have small lines in your journal. Your inner child needs more space to write. Be patient and kind as your child attempts to communicate with your adult self. Imagine that you are asking your five-year-old self what she wants to tell you as the adult. What does she want you to know or hear right now in your life?

Begin with: Dear (your name) . . .

Be open to whatever pops in your mind and write whatever comes up. There may be a question that your inner child asks your adult. If your adult wants to answer any questions, let your adult answer using your dominant hand with a normal pen. Allow a conversation to flow if that feels right. Be patient and be kind throughout the process.

*"No act of kindness, no matter how small, is ever wasted."*

—AESOP

## DAY SIX – DEVELOPING A KINDNESS ROUTINE

I really like this invitation: "In a world where you can be anything . . . be kind."

Today explore what a kindness routine would look like for you. It should include daily expressions of kindness for yourself, your family, people at work, and RAoK.

Here are a few more ideas to help develop a routine and stick to it:

- Make a decision.

- Set small goals for the routine.

- Make a plan.

- Be consistent with time.

- Be prepared.

- Make it fun and enjoyable.

- Track your progress.

- Reward yourself for a job well done.

_____

Journal about what this routine would look like for you and what small RAoK you could practice.

*"Be kind whenever possible. It is always possible."*
—THE FOURTEENTH DALAI LAMA

## DAY SEVEN – LOOKING BACK AND MOVING FORWARD

- Today look back over the week and journal about your kindness routine and how often you practiced RAoK.

- How did it feel?

- Try to really explore in writing how it felt to be more kind to yourself and others.

*Saying YES!*

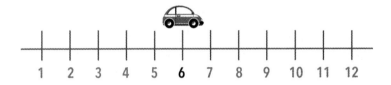

| | | | | | | | | | | | |
|1|2|3|4|5|**6**|7|8|9|10|11|12|

*"Realize deeply that the present moment is all you ever have. Make the Now the primary focus of your life."*
—ECKHART TOLLE

## DAY ONE – EXPLORING SAYING YES

A wonderful way to start saying *yes* to life is through exploring some of the findings of positive psychology. Professor Christopher Peterson defines positive psychology this way: "Positive psychology is the scientific study of what makes life most worth living."

It focuses on strengths instead of weakness in human thoughts, feelings, and behavior; it builds on the good in life instead of repairing the bad. It focuses on the positive events and experiences like joy, inspiration, and love—on positive traits like gratitude and compassion. It looks at character strengths like optimism, self-compassion, and life satisfaction. Basically it is a way to learn how to help yourself flourish instead of focusing on what is wrong in your life.

Sonja Lyubomirsky, a professor of psychology and a leader in the field of positive psychology, lists six habits of happy people:

- Be grateful.
- Look on the bright side.
- Savor the moment.
- Exercise.
- Meditate.
- Cultivate relationships.

---

Today choose one of these habits (or more if you'd like) and write about how you incorporate that habit in your life already and then explore how you can incorporate it even more.

*yes is a world*
*and in this world of*
*yes live*
*(skillfully curled)*
*all worlds*

—E. E. CUMMINGS

## DAY TWO – PRACTICING HEALTHY HABITS

- What makes you happy?

- List ten things off the top of your head that you enjoy doing that make you feel good.

- Looking back over the list of the six habits of happy people, how often do you practice any of those habits?

- Write each one of the habits, and next to it, write one thing you could do every day this week.

*"You are a living magnet. What you attract into your life is in harmony with your dominant thought and visions."*

—BRIAN TRACY

## DAY THREE – CREATIVE VISUALIZATION

Today's visualization is about saying *yes* to life.

Joseph Campbell, author of *The Hero's Journey*, believes that the warrior's approach is to say yes to life—yes to it all—and explains that we cannot cure the world of sorrows, but we can choose to live in joy. So today you will explore how it might feel to say *yes* to life, *yes* to it all.

When you are finished, acknowledge the process in whatever way feels comfortable for you. Perhaps use Shakti Gawain's words from her book *Creative Visualization*:

This or something better,
now manifests for me
in totally satisfying and harmonious ways,
for the highest good of all concerned.

The complete visualization can be found on my YouTube page: go to https://www.youtube.com/user/PattiKClark

Now Journal:

- Write it all out. Just begin free-flow to describe your experience.

- What did you see? What did you feel? What was your experience?

- Just allow the free-flow writing to express the experience of the visualization.

*"Sometimes saying yes is simply a leap of faith . . . Start with a yes, and see where that takes you . . . Say yes and you'll figure it out afterwards."*
—TINA FEY

## DAY FOUR – EXPRESSIVE WRITING

Here we go—remember, expressive writing comes from innermost thoughts and feelings, just let it flow.

- Write for a minimum of fifteen minutes.
- Write continuously: do not worry about punctuation, spelling, and grammar. If you run out of things to say, write that—that you don't know what to say—but don't stop writing. Keep pen on paper.
- Write a sentence or a few about each prompt.
- Write about how you feel when you complete the exercise. What does it bring up for you?

---

Today's Prompt:

- The best thing that happened today was . . .
- The best thing that happened this week was . . .
- The best thing that happened this year was . . .
- The best thing that happened in my life was . . .

*"The purpose of life, after all, is to live it, to taste experience to the utmost, to reach out eagerly and without fear for newer and richer experience."*
—ELEANOR ROOSEVELT

## DAY FIVE – LETTER TO SELF

Read about the five elements of well-being as described by Martin Seligman:

Psychologist Martin Seligman is credited as the father of Positive Psychology. In his book *Flourish*, Seligman described the five elements of well-being. Today's focus will be on Seligman's PERMA Model. This helps us think about what we need to do to flourish—and move toward happiness as a result:

**Positive Emotion (P)**—For us to experience well-being, we need positive emotion in our lives. Any positive emotion such as joy, gratitude, serenity, interest, hope, pride, amusement, inspiration, awe, and love fit this category. The message is simple: it's important to enjoy yourself now, in the present moment.

**Engagement (E)**—When we're fully engaged in a situation or project, we experience a state of flow, we lose our sense of self, time seems to stop, and we are focused on the present. The more we are able to experience this type of engagement, the better we feel.

**Positive Relationships (R)**—Having positive relationships is a universal requirement to well-being. People who have meaningful, positive relationships with others have a sense of community and are happier than those who do not.

**Meaning (M)**—Belonging to and serving something you believe is bigger than yourself. (Service and helping others.)

**Accomplishment (A)**—Pursuing success, winning, achievement, and mastery for their own sake.

With PERMA in mind, write a letter to yourself about how you intend to incorporate more of these elements in your life to help yourself flourish.

212 | RECOVERY ROAD TRIP

*"Sometimes we receive the power to say yes to life.*
*Then peace enters us and makes us whole."*
—RALPH WALDO EMERSON

## DAY SIX – TRYING SOMETHING NEW … WATCH AND DO

Try something new for thirty days—Matt Cutts TED Talk:

https://www.youtube.com/watch?
v=JnfBXjWm7hc&t=160s&ab_channel=TED

---

After watching this TED Talk, journal for a few minutes about what came up for you as you watched it. And write about how you might practice trying something new.

*"Always say yes to the present moment. What could be more futile, more insane, than to create inner resistance to what already is? What could be more insane than to oppose life itself, which is now and always now? Surrender to what is. Say yes to life . . . and see how life suddenly starts working for you rather than against you."*

—ECKHART TOLLE

## DAY SEVEN – LOOKING BACK AND MOVING FORWARD

Congratulations, you completed week six and are halfway through the journaling process.

---

- Look back over the past six weeks, read your journal entries, and write free-flow about what came up for you as you read it.

- Did you notice any changes in your attitude as the weeks progressed?

- Really check in with yourself, praise yourself for as much as you've done (even if it is not as much as you think you "should" be doing.)

- Make a commitment to keep going for the next six weeks.

*Forgiveness*

WEEK 7

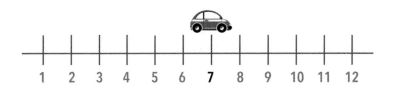

1   2   3   4   5   6   **7**   8   9   10   11   12

*"Forgiveness is the great 'yes'. It is a decision in the sense that you have to will it. You have to choose life. A person can choose death by not forgiving. So there is a sense in which you can destroy yourself by not saying yes to the reality that actually exists. That's the choice, yes or no to what truly exists."*

—FATHER THOMAS HOPKO

## DAY ONE – EXPLORING THE IDEA OF FORGIVENESS

That link between saying yes to what is and forgiveness is closely linked. So this week we will explore forgiveness and the choice to saying yes or no to what truly exists.

Today, think about the idea of forgiveness. Perhaps you are a person who finds it easy to forgive and notices the many benefits from this. For others, the term forgiveness may bring up old religious dogma or perhaps the whole idea is just repugnant for you. If you do have a problem with the idea of forgiveness, don't let that get in the way of these powerful exercises this week.

- What thoughts come up when you think about forgiveness? Write everything that pops into your head.

- Write about past experiences you have had with forgiveness —both you forgiving others and others forgiving you.

- Do you find it easy or hard to forgive others?

- How about forgiving yourself?

*"People in general would rather die than forgive. It's that hard. If God said in plain language, 'I'm giving you a choice, forgive or die,' a lot of people would go ahead and order their coffin."*

—SUE MONK KIDD

## DAY TWO – PRACTICING FORGIVENESS

But why should we practice forgiveness? What is the point? The benefits of forgiving yourself and others are many. The Mayo Clinic considers forgiveness a key in moving forward on the path of physical, emotional, and spiritual well-being:

Generally, forgiveness is a decision to let go of resentment and thoughts of revenge. The act that hurt or offended you might always remain a part of your life, but forgiveness can lessen its grip on you and help you focus on other, more positive parts of your life. Forgiveness doesn't mean that you deny the other person's responsibility for hurting you, and it doesn't minimize or justify the wrong. You can forgive the person without excusing the act. Forgiveness brings a kind of peace that helps you go on with life. Letting go of grudges and bitterness can make way for happiness, health and peace. Forgiveness can lead to:

- Healthier relationships.
- Greater spiritual and psychological well-being.
- Less anxiety, stress, and hostility.
- Lower blood pressure.
- Fewer symptoms of depression.
- Stronger immune system.
- Improved heart health.
- Higher self-esteem.

---

Read through the list above.

- Which points stand out for you? Why?

- Is there someone that you believe you can never forgive? Why?

- Is there anything that you feel you can't forgive yourself for? Explore that.

*"Forgiveness means it finally becomes unimportant that you hit back.
You're done. It doesn't necessarily mean that you want to have lunch with
the person. If you keep hitting back, you stay trapped in the nightmare."*
—ANNE LAMOTT

## DAY THREE – CREATIVE VISUALIZATION

Marianne Williamson believes that "the practice of forgiveness is our most important contribution to the healing of the world." Today's visualization is about the practice of forgiveness in healing our self and ultimately contributing to healing the world.

You will go back to your Creative Space. In that space, you will explore forgiving yourself and others. This is a powerful and healing meditation and visualization.

When you are finished, acknowledge the process in whatever way feels comfortable for you. Perhaps use Shakti Gawain's words from her book *Creative Visualization*:

This or something better,
now manifests for me
in totally satisfying and harmonious ways,
for the highest good of all concerned.

The complete visualization can be found on my YouTube page: go to https://www.youtube.com/user/PattiKClark

Now Journal:

- Write it all out. Just begin free-flow to describe your experience.

- What did you see? What did you feel? What was your experience?

- Just allow the free-flow writing to express the experience of the visualization.

*"The act of forgiveness takes place in our own mind.*
*It really has nothing to do with the other person."*

—LOUISE HAY

## DAY FOUR – EXPRESSIVE WRITING

- Remember, expressive writing comes from innermost thoughts and feelings, just let it flow.

- Write for a minimum of fifteen minutes.

- Write continuously: do not worry about punctuation, spelling, and grammar. If you run out of things to say, write that—that you don't know what to say—but don't stop writing. Keep pen on paper.

- Choose one prompt and write about it at length or write a bit about each prompt.

---

Today's Prompt:

- I am angry and finding it hard to forgive _____ because . . .

- I could find it easier to forgive if . . .

- One thing that I need to forgive myself for is . . .

- One thing I am willing to do to come to a place of forgiveness toward another person is . . .

- One thing I am willing to do to come to a place of forgiveness toward myself is . . .

*"It's toughest to forgive ourselves. So it's probably best to start with other people. It's almost like peeling an onion. Layer by layer, forgiving others, you really do get to the point where you can forgive yourself."*

—PATTY DUKE

## DAY FIVE – EXPLORING FORGIVENESS: LETTER TO SELF

- Write a letter to yourself—explore feelings of forgiving others and ultimately yourself.

- Describe in this letter what act or behavior you find "unforgivable" in someone else . . . and in yourself.

- Express to yourself that you are worthy of forgiveness—like you would to a good friend who is feeling lost and unforgivable.

- Explore in this letter what you can do, what action you can take to make peace with another and with yourself to allow change.

*"The weak can never forgive. Forgiveness is the attribute of the strong."*

—MAHATMA GANDHI

## DAY SIX – DEVELOPING A ROUTINE OF FORGIVENESS

Practice forgiveness toward someone today, even if it is only in writing in your journal. The key to developing any trait in your life is to make it a daily practice. If anyone apologizes to you today, accept the apology graciously.

- Choose someone that you have had difficulty forgiving. Journal about why it is hard; what is the sticking point?

- Be rigorous in your journaling around this. Try to unearth what any resistance is about. If it is fear, what are you fearful of? What is the worst that can happen? Explore this.

- See if you can get to a point of forgiveness with this person. And if you can see if there is any way of opening up a discussion around this. You may not be able to move forward with this today or in the near future, but be open to the possibility.

- Is your side of the street clean in this relationship? Do you owe an apology too? Explore that in writing. Be open to any ideas of a way forward.

*"It's one of the greatest gifts you can give yourself, to forgive.*
*Forgive everybody."*
—MAYA ANGELOU

## DAY SEVEN – LOOKING BACK AND MOVING FORWARD

You are finished with week seven. Practicing forgiveness can be very difficult. Congratulations for persevering.

---

- Journal about what has been most challenging this week and why.

- Have your thoughts about forgiveness changed since the beginning of the week? If yes, how have they changed?

- There is a saying in recovery circles that "all we can do is *keep our side of the street clean.*" What can you do from today on to keep your side of the street clean.

- Remember what Gerald G. Jampolsky says: "Inner peace can be reached only when we practice forgiveness."

*Intention*

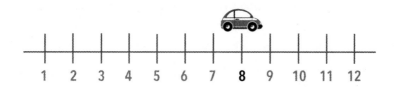

1   2   3   4   5   6   7   **8**   9   10   11   12

*"Intention gives attention direction."*
—DEEPAK CHOPRA

## DAY ONE – EXPLORING INTENTION

Deepak Chopra believes that intention is the starting point of every dream; that it is the creative power that fulfills all of our needs. He states that absolutely everything that happens in the universe begins with intention.

So why is it important to set intentions? Many thought leaders believe that this allows you to really focus on and live according to your values. Intentions give you purpose and the inspiration and motivation to achieve your purpose.

So this week we will explore becoming more intentional.

- What does it mean to you to be intentional?

- Do you make conscious intentions on a daily basis?

- This week try making at least one intention for the day each morning before you get out of bed. These intentions should have more of a focus on the present rather than future type goals, like trying to be kinder or more patient that day.

- Write a list of a few intentions that you'd like to explore this week.

*"Intention determines outcome. And if you're stuck and not moving forward, you have to check the thought and the action that created the circumstance."*

—OPRAH WINFREY

## DAY TWO – PRACTICING THE USE OF INTENTION

Many of us are adept at setting goals. Goal setting can help us focus on the future, help us determine what we want and create a plan, and then helps us stay on track to get there. But this can prevent us from being present in the moment and has a tendency to keep us focused on the future. Whereas setting intentions helps us focus on who we are in the present moment and live according to our values. Setting intentions daily can help to remind us how we want to behave each day; it can help us to focus on our deeper purpose and can inspire us to move toward that purpose. Intentions are about who you want to be and what you wish to contribute to the world.

---

- Today journal about your deeper purpose. Explore who you are in the present moment.

- Who do you want to be in this world?

- What do you want to contribute to the world?

*"The clearer and stronger your intention,*
*the more quickly and easily your creative visualization will work."*

—SHAKTI GAWAIN

## DAY THREE – CREATIVE VISUALIZATION

Today's visualization is about Intention.

Gary Zukav explains that the more aware of your intentions and your experiences you become, the more you will be able to connect the two, and the more you will be able to create the experiences of your life consciously. So today you will explore how to set intentions and live life more consciously.

When you are finished, acknowledge the process in whatever way feels comfortable for you. Perhaps use Shakti Gawain's words from her book *Creative Visualization*:

This or something better,
now manifests for me
in totally satisfying and harmonious ways,
for the highest good of all concerned.

The complete visualization can be found on my YouTube page: go to https://www.youtube.com/user/PattiKClark

---

Now Journal:

- Write it all out. Just begin free-flow to describe your experience.

- What did you see? What did you feel? What was your experience?

- Just allow the free-flow writing to express the experience of the visualization.

*Live with intention.*
*Walk to the edge.*
*Listen Hard.*
*Practice wellness.*
*Play with abandon.*
*Laugh.*
*Choose with no regret.*
*Appreciate your friends.*
*Continue to learn.*
*Do what you love.*
*Live as if this is all there is.*

—MARY ANNE RADMACHER

## DAY FOUR – EXPRESSIVE WRITING

- Remember, expressive writing comes from innermost thoughts and feelings, just let it flow.

- Write for a minimum of fifteen minutes.

- Write continuously: do not worry about punctuation, spelling, and grammar. If you run out of things to say, write that—that you don't know what to say—but don't stop writing. Keep pen on paper.

- Choose one prompt and write about it at length or write a bit about each prompt.

Today's Prompt:

- Living with intention means . . .

- I nurture my soul by . . .

- Every day I can live more intentionally by . . .
- My deepest purpose is . . . and I can move toward it by . . .

*"Intention is not something you do, but rather a force that exists in the universe as an invisible field of energy—a power that can carry us. It's the difference between motivation and inspiration. Motivation is when you get hold of an idea and don't let go of it until you make it a reality. Inspiration is the reverse—when an idea gets hold of you and you feel compelled to let that impulse or energy carry you along. You get to a point where you realize that you're no longer in charge, that there's a driving force inside you that can't be stopped. Look at the great athletes, musicians, artists, and writers. They all tap into a source."*

—WAYNE DYER

## DAY FIVE – LETTER TO SELF

Meg learned about intention at The Kripalu Center in Chapter 11. Tara Brach describes mindfulness of intention:

'One of the most powerful spiritual practices in the world is to reflect on your heart's deepest intention. There is a vast difference between ego-based intentions that perpetuate thoughts, feelings and actions that keep us imprisoned in feeling separate and limited, as opposed to remembering our deeper intentions, which call us home to the freedom of our true nature. This is the practice of mindfulness of intention. When you become aware of intention before you act, you are able to make wise choices that lead you to clarity, well-being, and harmony. Think about it, you can do the very same act, and do it out of resentment or frustration, with the intention to just get it over with, or it can be done with the desire to be present, to connect in a caring or loving way. These two ways of doing the same act produce very different results. Whenever you become mindful of your intentions, you have greater freedom to decide how you want to act. Your intentions have a powerful impact on others, and these intentions help to shape their response in turn. This is why it is so valuable to mindfully pause; always take a breath and check in with your intention before you act.'

- Write a letter to yourself supporting you to live by your deepest intentions, to support yourself in the practice of "mindful intention."

- Write to support yourself to be more present, to have more freedom to decide how you want to act in every interaction.

- Write about your desire to support yourself to live more intentionally.

*"The best way to ensure you achieve the greatest satisfaction out of life is to behave intentionally."*

—DEBORAH DAY

## DAY SIX – A ROUTINE OF INTENTIONALITY

Developing a routine of intentionality helps you focus on being present and living by your values. So today, write about how you can develop a routine of becoming more intentional on a daily basis.

Here are a few ways to become more intentional:

1. Say one intention each morning before you get out of bed.
2. Choose to be kind to people you encounter each day.
3. Pause and ask why you are doing something before you do it.
4. Make time for self-reflection.
5. Do something each day you are proud of.

Make your own list of ways that you will be more intentional and describe how you will make it a routine.

> *"Our intention creates our reality."*
> —WAYNE DYER

## DAY SEVEN – LOOKING BACK AND MOVING FORWARD

Let's explore the idea from day three: Gary Zukav explains that the more aware of your intentions and your experiences you become, the more you will be able to connect the two, and the more you will be able to create the experiences of your life consciously.

---

- Has this week helped you become more aware of the connection between your intentions and your experiences?

- Do you believe that awareness of this connection enables you to create the experiences of your life more consciously? Explore that concept.

- Have the exercises this week helped you develop a routine of more intentional living?

- Write about why you will keep developing this routine or why you don't think it has made much of difference. Explore that.

*Gratitude*

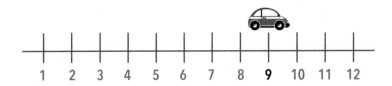

1  2  3  4  5  6  7  8  **9**  10  11  12

## DAY ONE – EXPLORING GRATITUDE

Most of us are well aware of the benefits of gratitude. As we take time to notice and appreciate the people, things, and events that we are thankful for, we experience more positive emotions, feel more alive, and experience more compassion; we tend to get better sleep, our bodies tend to be healthier, with stronger immune systems.

Throughout this journaling process, we have looked at the benefits of having a routine to develop new habits. So this week you'll be beginning the routine of making a gratitude list. Maybe this is something you've done before or maybe this is just the beginning. If you are just starting, this practice can be life changing.

This is a great practice to do first thing in the morning. You can write in this journal or you can start a new journal that is only for your gratitude, a stand-alone gratitude journal.

---

- Start by listing three things or people that you are grateful for.

- Write as much as you can about why you are grateful for that person or that thing.

- You'll be listing three new things each day this week. The more fully you write about why you are grateful, the better.

- As Marcus Tullius Cicero reminds us: "Gratitude is not only the greatest of virtues, but the parent of all others."

*"Gratitude for the present moment
and the fullness of life now is the true prosperity."*
—ECKHART TOLLE

## DAY TWO – PRACTICING GRATITUDE

Hopefully you've already begun the practice yesterday by writing down the three things that you are grateful for. And hopefully you started your day today by writing down three more.

As Meg learned in Northampton, gratitude helps you to grow your awareness of the good things in life and overcome the brain's negativity bias, which tends to spot what is wrong before it notices what is right. Robert Emmons, the world's leading scientific expert on gratitude, lists several compelling reasons why we should practice gratitude on a daily basis:

- Physical: Stronger immune systems; less bothered by aches and pains; lower blood pressure; and sleep longer and feel more refreshed upon waking

- Psychological: Higher levels of positive emotions; more alert, alive, and awake; more joy and pleasure; more optimism and happiness

- Social: More helpful, generous, and compassionate; more forgiving; more outgoing; feel less lonely and isolated.

- Take a minute and decide, which of the points above do you want to focus on? The desire to improve in that area will help drive you to continue in the practice.

- Explore that area and write about it.

- Write about times that you remember feeling especially grateful. Notice how your body feels as you remember that time.

*"What you radiate outward in your thoughts, feelings, mental pictures, and words, you attract into your life."*
—CATHERINE PONDER

## DAY THREE – CREATIVE VISUALIZATION

Today's visualization is about gratitude.

Amy Collette believes that gratitude is a powerful catalyst for happiness, that it is the spark that lights a fire of joy in your soul. Today, you will explore the power of gratitude and the benefits that it offers, including the possibility to spark joy. This visualization has the potential to change your life.

When you are finished, acknowledge the process in whatever way feels comfortable for you. Perhaps use Shakti Gawain's words from her book *Creative Visualization*:

This or something better,
now manifests for me
in totally satisfying and harmonious ways,
for the highest good of all concerned.

The complete visualization can be found on my YouTube page: go to https://www.youtube.com/user/PattiKClark

---

Now Journal:

- Write it all out. Just begin free-flow to describe your experience.

- What did you see? What did you feel? What was your experience?

- Just allow the free-flow writing to express the experience of the visualization.

*"Gratitude is an antidote to negative emotions, a neutralizer of envy, hostility, worry, and irritation. It is savoring; it is not taking things for granted; it is present-oriented."*

—SONJA LYUBOMIRSKY

## DAY FOUR – EXPRESSIVE WRITING

- Remember, expressive writing comes from innermost thoughts and feelings, just let it flow.
- Write for a minimum of fifteen minutes.
- Write continuously: do not worry about punctuation, spelling, and grammar. If you run out of things to say, write that—that you don't know what to say—but don't stop writing. Keep pen on paper.
- Choose one prompt and write about it at length or write a bit about each prompt.

---

Today's Prompt:

- I am most grateful about . . .
- Five things I am grateful for are. . .
- I practice gratitude by . . .
- I express gratitude by . . .

*"Develop an attitude of gratitude, and give thanks for everything that happens to you, knowing that every step forward is a step toward achieving something bigger and better than your current situation."*

—BRIAN TRACY

## DAY FIVE – LETTER TO SELF

- Write a heartfelt letter to yourself expressing your deep gratitude for who you are and what you have done so far in your life.

- Write this letter as you would to a dear friend, a sincere, loving thank-you letter.

*"The struggle ends when the gratitude begins."*
—NEALE DONALD WALS

## DAY SIX – GRATITUDE ON A DAILY BASIS

In Northampton, Meg learned about overcoming negativity bias—the idea that the human psyche is more affected by negative things than by those that are positive. The effect of the negativity bias is that even if positive things are happening around you, the negative things usually dominate your thinking and emotions; the human brain has a natural negativity bias to internalize negative experiences more deeply than positive ones. And practicing gratitude on a daily basis can interrupt or offset that bias. But the positive experiences and gratitude for them have to be focused on deliberately and consciously in order for them to really sink in. It takes five positive interactions to make up for a single negative interaction, and to really absorb a positive experience, it must be focused on for at least fifteen seconds.

---

- Today your task is to pause and take the time to let any positive experiences sink in, and then to express gratitude about that positive experience.

- If you see a beautiful flower or hear a lovely birdcall, pause, appreciate it, and take the time to express gratitude for it.

- And if someone says something nice to you, pause, take it in, and say thank you.

- In your journal, write about that experience. Did it come naturally? Was it awkward? Did you enjoy it?

- Make a commitment to this practice, in writing. Try to do this every day for the next two weeks and write about the experience.

*"'Thank you' is the best prayer that anyone could say. I say that one a lot. Thank you expresses extreme gratitude, humility, understanding."*

—ALICE WALKER

## DAY SEVEN – LOOKING BACK AND MOVING FORWARD

Congratulations, you have finished week nine. Hopefully you found this week uplifting. And hopefully you feel inspired to keep going with your gratitude journal. It is a transformational life practice.

---

- Before you journal today, look back over the past week of journal entries, what do you notice?

- Did you take time to pause to try to offset the negativity bias?

- Did you add to your gratitude journal every day?

- Today, journal about what stood out for you this week.

- Did you notice that your mood improved when you deliberately practiced gratitude?

- Make a commitment in writing to continue with this practice. Of all the tools offered here, I truly believe this one is the most transformational.

*Creativity*

1  2  3  4  5  6  7  8  9  **10**  11  12

*"You can't use up creativity. The more you use, the more you have."*

—MAYA ANGELOU

## DAY ONE – EXPLORING CREATIVITY AND WHY WE ALL NEED IT

This week the focus is on creativity. We always hear about the importance of practicing creativity in our daily lives, but why? What is the point?

In 2018, a study was done showing that creative arts of any kind can help stress and can be a healthy outlet in dealing with depression (US National Library of Medicine).

Practicing any form of creativity has been shown to reduce anxiety, depression, and stress and can help to process trauma.

---

- Today, write about the role that creativity plays in your life.

- Do you have a regular creative outlet?

- Do you generally let your creativity flourish, or do you stifle your creativity?

- Today, make a list of all the ways you practice creativity. Remember creativity can show up in many different ways: gardening, writing, music, drawing, doodling, painting, pottery, sculpting, dance, poetry, cooking, sewing, designing things, building—the list is vast. Now add to this list. What creative activity would you like to try this week?

- Make a commitment in writing to try at least one new creative activity this week. And after you try it, write about it.

*"Creativity takes courage."*

—HENRI MATISSE

## DAY TWO – THE COURAGE TO PRACTICE CREATIVITY

Expressing your creativity takes immense courage; it takes courage to express the things you are passionate about, and courage to risk being judged for what you create. But many studies have determined that repressed creativity leads to anxiety and depression. Douglas Eby, author of the *Creative Mind* series, believes that repressed creativity expresses itself in unhealthy relationships, overwhelming stress, depression, severe neurotic or even psychotic behavior, and addictive behaviors such as alcoholism. So although it takes courage to practice creativity, it is important to feel that fear and do it anyway.

Today, watch this TED Talk: "A Powerful Way to Unleash Your Natural Creativity" https://www.ted.com/talks/tim_harford_a_powerful_way_to_unleash_your_natural_creativity?language=en

---

- Journal about your thoughts on the talk.

- Journal about any fear you have of around getting creative. Be honest.

- Explore any creative desires you may have had but perhaps stifled due to fear.

- Write about how you can overcome any fears that may be blocking you. The fears may be illogical, but give yourself permission to write it out and explore it.

*"Imagination is the beginning of creation. You imagine what you desire,*
*you will what you imagine and at last you create what you will."*
—GEORGE BERNARD SHAW

## DAY THREE – CREATIVE VISUALIZATION

Today's visualization is about creativity.

Brené Brown believes that the only unique contribution that we will ever make in this world will be born of our creativity. So today you will explore creativity in the fullest sense and how to feel more creatively inspired to make your own unique contribution to the world.

When you are finished, acknowledge the process in whatever way feels comfortable for you. Perhaps use Shakti Gawain's words from her book *Creative Visualization*:

This or something better,
now manifests for me
in totally satisfying and harmonious ways,
for the highest good of all concerned.

The complete visualization can be found on my YouTube page: go to https://www.youtube.com/user/PattiKClark

Now Journal:

- Write it all out. Just begin free-flow to describe your experience.

- What did you see? What did you feel? What was your experience?

- Just allow the free-flow writing to express the experience of the visualization.

*"The creative process is a process of surrender, not control."*

—JULIA CAMERON

## DAY FOUR – EXPRESSIVE WRITING

Pennie Brownlee, author of *Magic Places*, describes the surrender process: "In other words, the creator surrenders to the creative energy live streaming through her. Pablo Picasso recognized this when he said, 'Every child is an artist. The problem is how to remain an artist once he grows up.'"

Take this quote about the process of surrender and surrendering to the creative energy live streaming through you and explore this in expressive writing.

- Remember, expressive writing comes from innermost thoughts and feelings, just let it flow.

- Write for a minimum of fifteen minutes.

- Write continuously: do not worry about punctuation, spelling, and grammar. If you run out of things to say, write that—that you don't know what to say—but don't stop writing. Keep pen on paper.

- Choose one prompt and write about it at length or write a bit about each prompt.

---

Today's Prompt:

- I surrender by . . .

- I can allow creative energy to live stream more easily by . . .

- Surrendering to the process is easy/difficult for me because . . .

- I can practice more creativity today by . . .

*"But unless we are creators, we are not fully alive. What do I mean by creators? Not only artists, whose acts of creation are the obvious ones of working with paint of clay or words. Creativity is a way of living life, no matter our vocation or how we earn our living. Creativity is not limited to the arts or having some kind of important career."*

—MADELEINE L'ENGLE

## DAY FIVE – LETTER TO SELF

- Write a letter supporting yourself in exploring your creative endeavors.

- Write the letter as you would to a dear friend who was looking to embark on a journey exploring her creativity.

- Encourage you to explore creativity as a way of living life no matter how you earn your living. Encourage yourself to be bold.

*"The worst enemy to creativity is self-doubt."*
—SYLVIA PLATH

## DAY SIX – CREATIVITY AND NATURE

Today go for a walk. Walking with intention is a wonderful way to open yourself up to creativity. And being out in nature is good for you.

Frederick Law Olmsted, landscape architect of the 1800s, has a brilliant quote: "Nature employs the mind without fatigue and yet enlivens it. Tranquilizes it and enlivens it. And thus, through the influences of the mind over body, gives the effect of refreshing rest and reinvigoration to the whole system."

Research has backed that beautiful quote. Being in nature calms us; it helps to lower our blood pressure, it soothes anxiety and helps elevate our mood. It helps us slow down our pace and appreciate the moment. And it leads to an experience of awe: that feeling we get when we encounter something vast and wondrous, that challenges our comprehension. Our jaw drops, and we naturally pause; our heart rate slows and we breathe more deeply. We tend to become more optimistic and can be more open to our creativity.

---

- So today, go for a walk in nature. Look for something in nature—a leaf, a shell, a flower.

- Go home and write about it, or sketch it, or write a song about it, or just hold it and take some uninterrupted time to look at it closely—the colors, the contours, the textures.

- Write about the experience in your journal.

*"Creativity is contagious, pass it on."*

—ALBERT EINSTEIN

## DAY SEVEN – LOOKING BACK AND MOVING FORWARD

Well done, you finished week ten. Hopefully you had a fun week exploring your creativity.

Today, watch one more TED Talk—this talk is one of the most popular talks ever given. It is by Sir Ken Robinson entitled: "Do Schools Kill Creativity."

https://www.ted.com/talks/sir_ken_robinson-
do_schools_kill_creativity

---

- Watch the talk and then write your thoughts about it.

- Go back and read through your journal entries. Did you try something new this week? Write about how it felt this week possibly being more open to your creativity.

*Exploring the
Sacred Feminine*

1  2  3  4  5  6  7  8  9  10  **11**  12

*"When we can remember and embody the Divine Feminine,
there is a place of total security within us, and when we live there,
we trust life because we have learned to trust ourselves."*

—ALICIA KEYS

## DAY ONE – EXPLORING THE SACRED FEMININE

What is meant by the idea "Sacred Feminine"? The Sacred Feminine is a term usually used when describing *an energy*. It is an energy within all of us that serves life itself. The qualities usually associated with Sacred Feminine energy are: unconditional love, compassion, wisdom, beauty, gentleness, patience, acceptance, forgiveness, nurturing, welcoming, accessibility, kindness, intuition, and healing. For women, embracing the Sacred Feminine energy is about embracing and trusting her intuition, standing in her power and helping to create a more harmonious world. This is the energy of the nurturer, the healer, and the compassionate one. Our culture has suppressed the Sacred Feminine. We've been encouraged to push, to do more, get more, to achieve above all else, but this leaves many of us stressed-out, depleted, and exhausted. We need to allow the Sacred Feminine to flourish within us.

---

- Today, journal about how Sacred Feminine energy exists in your life.

- Maybe do a bit of research and see what comes up.

- Does it feel familiar or strange? Is it something you feel comfortable with or does it feel awkward and outside your comfort zone.

- Write about it; explore these feelings.

*"The Sacred Feminine is not New Age. It is ageless and from the beginning. The Sacred Feminine is in our blood. It is our heritage. You have permission to say, 'God is Woman,' and 'God is Me.'"*

—ELIZABETH EILER

## DAY TWO – PRACTICING THE SACRED FEMININE

How do we practice the Sacred Feminine in everyday life? Much has been written about ways to connect with our Sacred Feminine energy. Here is a simple list of ways to start connecting today:

### LISTEN TO YOUR INTUITION

Check in with yourself when you are deciding what to do or have a decision you need to make. Close your eyes and take a breath—check in with your body. If you don't do this often, it may take some time, but listen closely. Feel if there is tension or ease around a project or action. Pay attention to the small, still voice inside. Write about the experience or do free-flow writing about what it felt like.

### TUNE IN TO YOUR BODY

This is closely aligned with number one. Check in with your body often throughout the day. Notice if your shoulders are tight or if your stomach is in knots. Roll your neck, lay on your back and stretch, do yoga. Your body will pass on messages at a deep level, ways to move forward, activities to do and those to avoid, about people who are positive forces in your life and those who are not.

### PAY ATTENTION TO YOUR WHOLE SELF, WARTS AND ALL

We often disregard the part of us that we consider "bad," "wrong," or "negative"—but our *shadow* side has much to teach us. We need to allow our shadow to teach us in order to become more fully integrated.

Ask your shadow to share what it would like to share with you. Listen and journal about what you learn.

## ASK QUESTIONS

One of the best ways to connect with our Sacred Feminine energy is get quiet and ask questions. Inquire deeply about your values and behavior. Ask why you believe what you believe. Ask why you do certain things. Inquire and be open to the answers.

## BE IN NATURE

Spending time in nature is one of the best ways to connect to this energy. In nature the feminine creative energy is ever present. Even a few minutes of fresh air outside is helpful; stand barefoot in the grass to connect with the Sacred Feminine. And whenever you can find the time, go walk on the beach or among trees, feel the Earth energy.

## MEDITATE

One of the quickest ways to connect with this energy is to get out of your head and drop into your heart. The Sacred Feminine is accessed most quickly when we get quiet and meditate. Tune in to the quiet and listen.

---

- Journal about these six suggestions for getting in touch with your Sacred Feminine energy. Take time and explore each one.

- See which one resonates best with you and practice that.

- Try to take time to practice each one this week.

- Journal about your experience.

*"Until women can visualize the sacred female they cannot be whole and society cannot be whole."*

—ELINOR GADON

## DAY THREE – CREATIVE VISUALIZATION

Today's visualization is about the Sacred Feminine.

Alicia Keys explains that when we embody the qualities of the Sacred Feminine we are empowered to fully engage in our lives. Today, you will explore the concept of the Sacred Feminine and how to live from that inspired place to fully engage in life.

When you are finished, acknowledge the process in whatever way feels comfortable for you. Perhaps use Shakti Gawain's words from her book *Creative Visualization*:

This or something better,
now manifests for me
in totally satisfying and harmonious ways,
for the highest good of all concerned.

The complete visualization can be found on my YouTube page: go to https://www.youtube.com/user/PattiKClark

---

Now Journal:

- Write it all out. Just begin free-flow to describe your experience.

- What did you see? What did you feel? What was your experience?

- Just allow the free-flow writing to express the experience of the visualization.

*"Who is She? She is your power, your Feminine source. Big Mama. The Goddess. The Great Mystery. The web-weaver. The life force. The first time, the twentieth time, you may not recognize her. Or pretend not to hear. As she fills your body with ripples of terror and delight. But when she calls, you will know you've been called. Then it is up to you to decide if you will answer."*

—LUCY H. PEARCE

## DAY FOUR – EXPRESSIVE WRITING

- Remember, expressive writing comes from innermost thoughts and feelings, just let it flow.

- Write for a minimum of fifteen minutes.

- Write continuously: do not worry about punctuation, spelling, and grammar. If you run out of things to say, write that—that you don't know what to say—but don't stop writing. Keep pen on paper.

- Choose one prompt and write about it at length or write a bit about each prompt.

---

Today's Prompt:

- Describe what Sacred Feminine means to you.

- I experience the Sacred Feminine as . . .

- I feel most powerful when I . . .

- My energy feels depleted when I . . .

*"In our path back to the Divine Feminine, everyone without exception is on the path of creativity. The source of all creativity is consciousness. The more consciousness you have, the more potential you have to create."*

—DEEPAK CHOPRA

## DAY FIVE – LETTER TO SELF

- Write a letter to yourself about how you can more deeply embrace your Sacred Feminine.

- Be supportive and let your intuition guide you in the letter.

*"The power of the Divine Feminine sustains all life on Earth, and we can make choices to bring that support into our own lives."*

—ALICIA KEYS

## DAY SIX – THE DAILY PRACTICE OF THE SACRED FEMININE

*Spirituality and Health Magazine* explores the daily practice of harnessing the power of the Sacred Feminine: "Humanity has neglected and disregarded the feminine for millennia. Embracing the Sacred Feminine is an indispensable contribution to the healing and transformation of the world."

Through honoring the Sacred Feminine, we find natural access to spiritual qualities like receptivity, patience, the ability to listen, and the care for life.

Here are some ideas from the article to help develop a daily practice of embracing your Sacred Feminine energy:

### DROP FROM YOUR HEAD INTO YOUR HEART

The energy of the feminine embodies the nurturer, the healer, the compassionate peacemaker. She makes choices from her heart, and compassion is her compass.

### CONNECT WITH NATURE

Spending more time with Mother Nature is one of the best ways to connect to this loving, omnipresent energy. In nature, the feminine creative energy runs wild. Its physical beauty is visible.

### FIND BALANCE

The Sacred Feminine is not about gender, as this energy lives in all of us, but much of our society operates from a masculine "hustle and do" mentality, which doesn't allow for much room to just be. The energies of action (masculine) and allowing (feminine) coexist, and we must find the balance between the two. Balance is key. When we find it, we are both taking inspired action and receiving and appreciating all of our desires.

### HONOR THE STILLNESS AND RECLAIM REST

The feminine energy revels in being. Many of us don't take enough time to relax, to literally revel in the art of doing nothing. Sit in silence for five minutes and observe what comes up for you. Taking time to be one with yourself in each moment can help you connect to the Sacred Feminine and divine light within.

### LIVE YOUR VALUES AND MAKE CHOICES WITH INTENTION

Invite yourself to push outside of your comfort zone. What can you do today that is new? How can you live with more integrity and make choices that honor your own soul's deepest desires? What have you always wanted to do but have not given yourself permission to do? Making conscious choices to enjoy new experiences will not only help you feel more balanced and joyful, it will help you harness the true power of the Sacred Feminine.

### PRACTICE SELF-LOVE AND COMPASSION

Self-love is misunderstood because it isn't a state of being but rather a decision you make when you finally realize that anything you experience is a direct reflection of your relationship with yourself. The ultimate way to embrace the Sacred Feminine is to practice self-love and embrace yourself fully. Start with loving yourself as you are, not as you think you should be. One of the biggest components to self-love is self-compassion. The relationship we have with ourselves sets the tone for everything in our life. Learning how to see yourself in the eyes of source energy is one of the best ways to live in the energy of the Sacred Feminine.

- Journal about these suggestions and commit to doing one of these this week.

*"They will want you seated, conformed, and quiet but don't you dare fit in. Scream the house down if it's what it will take to make your noise heard. The Divine Feminine has been shamed and shunned for self-expression for far too long; we aren't here to silence ourselves anymore."*

—NIKKI ROWE

## DAY SEVEN – LOOKING BACK AND MOVING FORWARD

Congratulations, you have completed week eleven. Only one more week to go.

---

- Today, go back and read your journal entries from this week. What stands out for you?

- Has your attitude about the Sacred Feminine energy changed at all?

- Journal about anything that you've learned about yourself this week.

*Bringing It All Together:*
*Moving Toward Living with*
*Greater Passion and Purpose*

1  2  3  4  5  6  7  8  9  10  11  **12**

*"Your purpose in life is to find your purpose and give your whole heart and soul to it."*
—BUDDHA

## DAY ONE – EXPLORING THE IDEA OF LIVING WITH GREATER PASSION AND PURPOSE

This is the last week of the workbook; as we bring our time together to a close, we'll focus on bringing everything we've learned about in the last eleven weeks together.

As Vincent Van Gogh says, "Great things are done by a series of small things brought together."

We'll also focus on how we can live with greater passion and purpose. Hopefully journaling for the past eleven weeks has helped in that pursuit. It has been said that passion and purpose go hand-in-hand, so when you are hoping to find your purpose, look to what brings you joy and evokes passion.

### WHAT DO YOU LOVE TO DO?

Identifying the things that you love to do is a great way to identify your passion and purpose. Go ahead, make a list; what do you love doing? Include everything that pops in your head. Don't edit, just let it flow. Notice what makes your pulse react. What do you get excited by? This list is your key to living with greater passion and purpose. Take time to let the list share its secrets with you. Make notes of what pops in your head when you look at the list.

### WHAT COMES EASILY TO YOU?

There is a saying—if you are pushing shit uphill, move out of the way and let it roll back down and take another trail. Explore what comes easily for you—this ties in with the suggestion above—usually if we love to do it, it comes more naturally to us. That ease is often a signal to our purpose. Look at what comes naturally to you and build on those strengths.

## LOOK BACK

Our history often gives us a clue to our way forward. What struggles have you overcome? What challenges have you successfully navigated? When you look back, what experiences charge you? What do you feel passionate about? This can be a clue toward your life purpose.

## PLAY

Explore possibilities like you did when you were a child. Think back to your childhood when you thought about what you might be when you grew up. What attracted you? During those daydreams we mostly just allowed our imagination to play. Open up to that child and see where she leads you.

## WHAT MAKES YOU HAPPY?

What gets you excited? What makes your pulse race? Identifying those things that set you on fire is usually connected to finding your passion. Identify what makes you happy and you will probably find the path to your purpose.

## FRIENDS AS MIRRORS

If you feel stuck even after exploring the above, perhaps ask a friend to be your mirror. We tend to be hard on ourselves and find it hard to identify our strengths. Friends can help identify your strengths and what you are good at. Ask them to mirror it back to you. Listen to what your friends see in you and let it sink in.

- Journal about the suggestions above.
- Make a few lists as suggested to explore ways to move forward.

*"Follow your dreams; they know the way."*

—KOBE YAMADA

## DAY TWO – IDENTIFYING PASSION AND PURPOSE

Watch the TED Talk: "How to Know Your Life Purpose in Five Minutes."

https://www.youtube.com/watch?v=vVsXO9brK7M

---

- Journal about the talk—what came up for you as you watched it?

*"There is no greater gift you can give or receive than to honor your calling. It's why you were born. And how you become most truly alive."*

—OPRAH WINFREY

## DAY THREE – CREATIVE VISUALIZATION

Today's visualization is about living with greater passion and purpose.

Wayne Dyer declares that when you focus on purpose and refuse to be discouraged by fear, you align with the infinite self, in which all possibilities exist. So today, for the final visualization of this workbook, you will explore purpose and what it feels like living life from a place of passion and purpose.

When you are finished, acknowledge the process in whatever way feels comfortable for you. Perhaps use Shakti Gawain's words from her book *Creative Visualization*:

This or something better,
now manifests for me
in totally satisfying and harmonious ways,
for the highest good of all concerned.

The complete visualization can be found on my YouTube page: go to https://www.youtube.com/user/PattiKClark

---

Now Journal:

- Write it all out. Just begin free-flow to describe your experience.

- What did you see? What did you feel? What was your experience?

- Just allow the free-flow writing to express the experience of the visualization.

*"My mission in life is not merely to survive, but to thrive; and to do so with some passion, some compassion, some humor, and some style."*

—MAYA ANGELOU

## DAY FOUR – EXPRESSIVE WRITING

- Remember, expressive writing comes from innermost thoughts and feelings, just let it flow.

- Write for a minimum of fifteen minutes.

- Write continuously: do not worry about punctuation, spelling, and grammar. If you run out of things to say, write that—that you don't know what to say—but don't stop writing. Keep pen on paper.

- Choose one prompt and write about it at length or write a bit about each prompt.

Today's Prompt:

- What did you imagine your life would be like when you were a small child?

- My biggest strengths are . . . My biggest weakness is . . .

- My biggest hope is . . . My biggest fear is . . .

- What I value most is . . . What gives my life most meaning is . . .

- I thrive when I . . .

- Moving forward, I choose to focus on . . .

*"I'm working on my own life story.*
*I don't mean I'm putting it together;*
*no, I'm taking it apart."*
—MARGARET ATWOOD

## DAY FIVE – LETTER TO SELF

- Write a letter to yourself encouraging you in finding your purpose.

- Write the letter as you would to a friend who is struggling in her search.

- Be compassionate and kind.

*"When you stay on purpose and refuse to be discouraged by fear, you align with the infinite self, in which all possibilities exist."*

—WAYNE DYER

## DAY SIX – ALIGNING WITH THE INFINITE SELF ON A DAILY BASIS

Watch this TED Talk: "Take Time, You'll Find Your Purpose in Life."

https://www.ted.com/talks/take_time_you_ll_find _your_purpose_in_life

---

- Journal about the TED talk. What did it bring up for you?
- Journal about the Wayne Dyer quote above. How can you align with your infinite self and avoid being discouraged by fear?

*"Believe in your heart that you're meant to live a life full of passion,*
*purpose, magic, and miracles."*
—ROY T. BENNETT

## DAY SEVEN – LOOKING BACK AND MOVING FORWARD

**Congratulations! You've done it!**
This is it, the final day of the final week!

Hopefully you have found the process of journaling for these twelve weeks helpful in moving toward living with more passion and purpose.

---

- Take time today to go back to day one, to the beginning of the journal.

- Use a highlighter and highlight statements and comments you wrote that stand out to you in some way.

- Journal today about what you notice after looking back; notes about any growth or changes you see in the twelve-week journey. This might take several sittings, be patient with this process and allow yourself time to really let it sink in.

- I encourage you to keep journaling, and I especially encourage you to believe that you are meant to live a life full of passion, purpose, magic, and miracles!

# Suggested Reading

**JOURNAL WRITING**

Christina Baldwin. Life's Companion: Journal Writing as a Spiritual Practice. Bantam Books, 2007.

Julia Cameron. The Artist's Way a Spiritual Path to Higher Creativity. Tarcher/Putnam, 2002.

Michael Bernard Beckwith. Lifevisioning: A Transformative Process for Activating Your Unique Gifts and Highest Potential. Sounds True, 2013.

**THE SACRED FEMININE**

Sue Monk Kidd. The Dance of the Dissident Daughter: A Woman's Journey from Christian Tradition to the Sacred Feminine. Harper One, 1996.

Clarissa Pinkola Estes. Women Who Run with the Wolves: Myths and Stories of the Wild Woman Archetype. New York: Ballantine Books, 1992.

**TRAUMA, ALCOHOL, WOMEN, AND HEALING**

Ann Dowsett Johnston. Drink: The Intimate Relationship between Women and Alcohol. Harper Wave, 2015.

Leah Odze Epstein and Caren Osten Gerszberg. Drinking Diaries: Women Serve Their Stories Straight Up. Seal Press, 2012.

Holly Whitaker. Quit like a Woman: The Radical Choice to Not Drink in a Culture Obsessed with Alcohol. The Dial Press, 2019.

Stephanie S. Covington. A Woman's Way through the Twelve Steps. Hazelden Publishing, 1994.

Mary Karr. Lit: A Memoir. Harper Perennial, 2010.

Anne Lamott. Rosie. Penguin Books, 1997.

Johann Hari. Chasing the Scream. Bloomsbury, 2016.

Gabor Maté and Peter A. Levine. In the Realm of Hungry Ghosts: Close Encounters with Addiction. North Atlantic Books, 2010.

## CREATIVITY

Betty Edwards. Drawing on the Right Side of the Brain. Tarcher, 2012.

Robert Root-Bernstein and Michèle Root-Bernstein. Sparks of Genius. Mariner Books, 2001.

Julia Cameron. *The Artist's Way*. Tarcher/Putnam, 1992.

## LOVE

Dalai Lama Xiv. Dalai Lamas Book of Love and Compassion. Thorsons, 2002.

Brené Brown. Gifts of Imperfection. Hazelden Publishing, 2010.

Brené Brown. Rising Strong: How the Ability to Reset Transforms the Way We Live, Love, Parent, and Lead. Random House, 2017.

Brené Brown. Braving the Wilderness: The Quest for True Belonging and the Courage to Stand Alone. Random House, 2019.

King, Vex. Good Vibes, Good Life: How Self-Love Is the Key to Unlocking Your Greatness. Hay House, 2018.

## UNITY

Anne Lamott. Almost Everything: Notes on Hope. Riverhead Books, 2018.

David Bradford and Carole Robin. Connect: Building Exceptional Relationships with Family, Friends, and Colleagues. Currency, 2021.

## COMPASSION

Kristin Neff. Self-Compassion: The Proven Power of Being Kind to Yourself. William Morrow Paperbacks, 2015.

Tara Brach. Radical Acceptance: Embracing Your Life with the Heart of a Buddha. Random House, 2004.

Tara Brach. Radical Compassion: Learning to Love Yourself and Your World with the Practice of RAIN. Penguin Life, 2020.

## KINDNESS

Angela Santomero. Radical Kindness. Harper Wave, 2019.

Danny Wallace. Random Acts of Kindness. Ebury, 2004.

## YES

Shonda Rhimes. Year of Yes: How to Dance It Out, Stand in the Sun and Be Your Own Person. Simon & Schuster, 2016.

Eckhart Tolle. The Power of Now: A Guide to Spiritual Enlightenment. New World Library, 2004.

Gabrielle Bernstein. Judgment Detox: Release the Beliefs That Hold You Back from Living a Better Life. Gallery Books, 2018.

## FORGIVENESS

Eva Mozes Kor. Power of Forgiveness. Central Recovery Press, 2021.

Gerald G. Jampolsky. Forgiveness: The Greatest Healer of All. Atria Books, 1999.

Adam Hamilton. Forgiveness: Finding Peace through Letting Go. Abingdon Press, 2012.

Colin Tipping. Radical Forgiveness. Sounds True, 2010.

Desmond Tutu. The Book of Forgiving. Harper One, 2015.

## INTENTION AND MEDITATION

Wayne W. Dyer. The Power of Intention: Learning to Co-Create Your World Your Way. Hay House, 2005.

Mallika Chopra. Living with Intent: My Somewhat Messy Journey to Purpose, Peace, and Joy. Harmony Books, 2016.

Jon Kabat-Zinn. Wherever You Go, There You Are: Mindfulness Meditation in Everyday Life. Hachette, 2005.

Jon Kabat-Zinn. Mindfulness for Beginners. Sounds True, 2006.

Pema Chodron. How to Meditate: A Practical Guide to Making Friends with Your Mind. Sounds True, 2007.

Jack Kornfield. Meditation for Beginners. Sounds True, 2008.

Salzberg, Sharon. Real Happiness: The Power of Meditation. Workman Publishing, 2010.

## GRATITUDE

Nancy Leigh Demoss. Choosing Gratitude. Moody Publishers, 2011.

Robert A. Emmons. Gratitude Works. Jossey-Bass, 2013.

Robert A. Emmons. Thanks!: How the New Science of Gratitude Can Make You Happier. Houghton Mifflin Co, 2007.

Oliver Sacks. Gratitude. Knopf, 2015.

Sarah Ban Breathnach. Simple Abundance: Journal of Gratitude. Grand Central Publishing, 2009.

# *Gratitudes*

I would like to thank the team at She Writes Press. To Brooke Warner especially, your support and guidance has meant the world to me.

I have such gratitude to my editors; they have done an amazing job at helping to make this book flow. Thank you to Krissa Lagos for your fine-tuning and support, your suggestions were so helpful, and to Lauren Wise for holding my hand through this process. And thank you to Annie Tucker for her fantastic editing and helpful advice. Annie, you are a gem! And big gratitude to my publicist Joanne McCall. You make the whole thing fun and I appreciate that more than I can say.

I am indebted to authors who have inspired me in my own life's journey: Tara Brach, Brené Brown, Julia Cameron, Anne Lamott, Gabor Maté, Caroline Myss, Stephanie Covington, Michael Beckwith, Shakti Gawain, Kristin Neff, and Johann Hari. There are so many more, but these few have been hugely impactful.

Such gratitude to the women I interviewed—past participants in my online workshops, as well as women I spoke to in 12-Step meetings. Thank you for sharing your lives with me. Many of your stories and experiences helped shape Meg and her journey.

Thank you so much to my friends Tam and Rosie for lending me your voices and inspiration for Nella and Rosie. I feel like both of you were on this journey with me.

Huge gratitude to my home group, my recovery family! The women and men in my home group are my support community, and I love each and every one of you.

Thank you to my book group for their support through this process. And a big thank you to my friends for their encouragement, for reading through early drafts of the book, sharing ideas, and for general enthusiasm: Rosie, Tam, Deb, Jeff, Jan, Ing, Nancy, and JaneE. A special thank you to JaneE for her courage, expertise, and wisdom reading the original first draft; her skillful recommendations changed the energy of the book in powerful and positive ways. And thank you to Deb for her suggestions helping to make the book feel more inclusive and accessible to all women, not only those in recovery.

A massive outpouring of gratitude to my son Devin for his help and skill in this process! He helped design my website and logo; he helped me create my videos for my YouTube page and get them uploaded and organized; and he did all of my author photographs. He embodies creativity!

Gratitude to my sister Karin for her lifelong inspiration and support, not only in recovery, but in every aspect of my life. And to my niece Chelsea for the wisdom and light she brings to the world.

I am so grateful to my sons Lukas and Devin—you two are my inspiration to be a better person every day. And I am so happy that they both have loving partners—so wonderful to see Alicia and Lukas and Fiona and Devin growing together and sharing their lives. What an incredible gift to see my sons so happy!

Massive thank you to my husband, Jeff (who is nothing like Meg's ex-husband!), for your love and support. You encouraged me and believed in me every step of the way. I am so grateful that we get to do this life together.

And finally, my ecstatic gratitude in welcoming Théodore Santiago to our family! And what immense joy it brings when I see Théodore being nurtured, witnessing firsthand how multigenerational trauma is being healed.

# About the Author

PATTI CLARK is the award-winning author of *This Way Up: Seven Tools for Unleashing Your Creative Self and Transforming Your Life*. She has also been featured on TVNZ's *Breakfast Show*, and her work has been featured in numerous publications, including *The Wall Street Journal*, *The Boston Globe*, *The Mindful Word*, and *Thrive Global*. Her own experience as a middle-aged woman in recovery is deeply reflected in this book, and is what inspired her to write it. Patti was born and raised in Northern California, lived in New Zealand for the past thirty years, and is now living in Portugal.

Photo credit: Devin Clark-Memler

## Looking for your next great read?

We can help!

Visit www.shewritespress.com/next-read
or scan the QR code below for a list
of our recommended titles.

She Writes Press is an award-winning
independent publishing company founded to
serve women writers everywhere.